THE SAVVY NEGOTIATOR

THE SAVVY NEGOTIATOR

Building Win-Win Relationships

William F. Morrison

PRAEGER

Westport, Connecticut
London

Library of Congress Cataloging-in-Publication Data

Morrison, William F. (William Fosdick), 1935–
    The savvy negotiator : building win/win relationships / William F. Morrison.
        p. cm.
    Includes bibliographical references and index.
    ISBN 0-275-98800-7 (alk. paper)
    1. Negotiation in business. 2. Negotiation. 3. Success in business. I. Title.
    HD58.6.M673 2006
    650.1'3—dc22   2005020943

British Library Cataloguing in Publication Data is available.

Library of Congress Catalog Card Number: 2005020943
ISBN: 0-275-98800-7

First published in 2006

Praeger Publishers, 88 Post Road West, Westport, CT 06881
An imprint of Greenwood Publishing Group, Inc.
www.praeger.com

Printed in the United States of America

The paper used in this book complies with the
Permanent Paper Standard issued by the National
Information Standards Organization (Z39.48-1984).

10 9 8 7 6 5 4 3 2 1

Books, as they should be, are dedicated to the very important people in the author's life. I dedicate this to the following VIPs:

When a father has a son and family that he can be very, very proud of, the father is a very happy man. I dedicate this book to:

William F. Morrison II
Jamie Morrison
Jack William Morrison

Other books by the author

The Prenegotiation Planning Book

John Wiley & Sons, Inc., 1985, First Edition
John Wiley & Sons, Inc., 1985, Second Edition
Krieger Publishing Company, 1992 (Reprint Edition)
Krieger Publishing Company, 2001 (Reprint Edition)

The Human Side of Negotiations

Krieger Publishing Company, 1994, First Edition

Contents

Acknowledgments

Family is the foundation of our lives and I want to acknowledge mine. These people, who are very important to me, provided material for this book and—significantly more important—the help and support necessary to finish a book while working a full-time job. My other children: Deanne, Donna, and Alaire. My other grandchildren: Benjamin, Brandon, Briana, Caleb, Chris, Joshua, Julia, Robbie, Ryan, and Sara. Also Janie and Jim Bender and Adam and Jerri McNamara, who live in Ohio. These wonderful people have been with me during the many good times in my life. They have also been there during the really bad times in my life and helped me move on. To all my family, thank you very much.

The list of people who have taught me and helped me to understand the process of negotiation is so long that it would fill a small book. Over 20,000 people have listened to me teach and talk about negotiations. Almost all of them have added to my knowledge of the subject, both during and after the formal class sessions. Several people deserve special mention.

Henry H. (Hank) Calero, who was the coauthor of my second book and who gave me a significant amount of information and raw data from his negotiation files for this book. He has spent most of his life studying negotiations, and the data and the understanding of the process that he gave me have been extremely valuable.

I had a wonderful second career at San Jose State University teaching in the College of Business (negotiation and other courses). This career would not have happened without the strong support of Marshall Bean, Burton Dean, Dave Denzler, Nancie Fimbel, Abdel El-Shaieb, Scott

Norwood, and Roger Salstrom. Each in his own way has been my mentor and teacher.

Behind every successful book is an editor who works behind the scenes helping pave the way as a book project goes through all the steps before it reaches the market. I have a wonderful editor, Nicholas Philipson.

Finally, Stan Wakefield, the agent who provided a major assist in bring this book to the public. I owe Stan a very big thank you for all his help and support.

Introduction

Dramatic changes took place during the last twenty years of the twentieth century in the way many negotiations are conducted and in the major objectives of the negotiation process. The purpose of this book is to review these changes, to support these changes, and to help readers maximize the outcome of their future negotiations in the twenty-first century.

First, negotiation changed from a process of conflict to a process of compromise; or to put it another way, from an adversarial process to a cooperative process. Up until the very late 1900s, the objective of most negotiators was to win (and win big) at the negotiation table. The negotiator wanted to be able to report to the principal or boss that the negotiator had won the negotiation. In the 2000s, negotiations will be judged more often by the outcome of the relationship started by the negotiation, rather than the outcome of the actual negotiation.

One simple example of the impact of this change comes from the sports world, comparing football to baseball. During the last few decades of the twentieth century, football became the national sport of the United States. For about 100 years, baseball had been the national pastime, but football became number one. Why? One significant reason is labor relations. Baseball had several major strikes and lockouts. One year the World Series was cancelled. The players did not trust the owners and the owners hated the players. Every negotiation was a win-lose negotiation. The players won almost all the time and they bragged that they won after each contract was signed. Baseball did not grow like football did during this period. The first contract negotiation without a strike occurred in

2002 (in the twenty-first century). Maybe both sides finally got it. By comparison, most of football's negotiations were certainly win-win oriented. There was labor peace and the sport grew, providing more income for both sides of the negotiation table.

Another change was the increase, especially in the United States, in the number of day-to-day negotiations for items we use at home and for our families. Previously, most people believed that the price tag gave the price and that was it. I cannot remember any time that my parents ever asked for a lower price when they purchased something. When purchasing autos, my father went to the same Chevrolet dealer for every car he purchased. My father knew that he was getting the right price. Looking back with twenty-twenty hindsight, I'm sure my father always paid too much.

In contrast, the *New York Times* reported in October 2002 that upscale stores in the city were negotiating prices for all their products with customers who asked for a better deal. The economy at that time was in a recession, but the pattern was being established for the future. Once customers learned they could negotiate for personal items, they could always negotiate for personal items.

Another consideration that I address is ethics. There are too many examples of unethical behavior in the late 1900s and early 2000s. Companies (e.g., Enron), universities (e.g., the University of Virginia), and people (e.g., Martha Stewart) are critically hurt because of their (un)ethical behavior. Ethics are a major part of the negotiation process. It is very difficult to negotiate a win-win contract with someone you do not trust or who does not trust you.

This book has two key objectives: first, to review the changes in the negotiation process in the twenty-first century and to discuss the key concepts for success in the future; second, to review the day-to-day negotiations that we should be involved in and to show how we can win these negotiations.

The foundation of this book is the Keys to Success that appear in every chapter. These form the basic learning objectives that are truly your keys to success in all your future negotiations. Throughout the book, important concepts are reviewed in depth. A Key to Success then follows most of these concepts to summarize them. These keys should be reviewed before every future negotiation.

Here is a blueprint for the book:

In chapter 1 there is a review of the past conflict centered negotiation process in both labor-management and buyer-seller negotiations. During this time, the only focus was winning at the negotiation table. The second half of the chapter introduces a new negotiation model with four truths that have been accepted as the basis for success in the twenty-first century. This chapter then reviews the significant changes in the negotiation process.

Chapter 2 introduces and explains in great detail several winning concepts that you must understand to be successful in the future. After reading this chapter you should have a basic understanding of the keys to winning future negotiations.

A very significant amount of time in every negotiation is spent asking and answering questions. To be successful negotiators must be highly skilled in this area of negotiations. Chapter 3 reviews twenty-seven different types of questions providing hints on how to be successful both asking and answering these questions. This chapter shows you the power of asking and answering questions in negotiations.

I'm very pleased that in society today there is significantly more emphasis on ethics and the need to improve our ethical behavior. Chapter 4 reviews a few current examples of unethical behavior. Then it looks at ethics and negotiations. The chapter closes with five questions you must answer, in any situation that could have ethical implications, BEFORE you act. Remember positive ethics will lead to positive negotiation results.

Included in chapter 5 are many examples of past negotiation situations in the day-to-day lives of people I know. The only purpose of this chapter is to convince you that it is okay to negotiate in your personal life and that you have the opportunity to make large savings when you do. The chapter will also help you identify opportunities to negotiate in your daily activities.

Most of the time when we think about negotiations we consider face-to-face negotiations. In the twenty-first century many negotiations are not face-to-face. Chapter 6 provides several hints to help you be more successful.

In the conclusion, I take a long look at the negotiation process providing insights that do not easily fit into the first six chapters. There is also a review of the positive behaviors of successful negotiators.

In this book, there are many "keys to success." These are listed by chapter in the appendix.

This book has a number of objectives. First, it provides a short review of the history of negotiations and how negotiations have changed over time. Then I look ahead to what the process will look like in the twenty-first century.

Second, it reviews a large number of key concepts that apply to all negotiations. These concepts have been proven over time and must be understood by all who negotiate. They must be part of every person's negotiation toolbox.

Third, it reviews seven basic winning concepts that apply to all negotiation situations that must be understood by people who negotiate no matter what the negotiation situation.

Fourth, it reviews several tactics commonly used in negotiations. This will allow you to identify when a negotiation tactic is being used and to proactively use negotiation tactics to achieve your objectives.

Fifth, it attempts to convince you that there are thousands of opportunities to improve your daily life by negotiating and using common negotiation techniques. Included in the text are a large number of examples of actual negotiations that my students and friends have reported to me. These range from negotiating the purchase of a mattress to negotiating with the upstairs neighbor who practices basketball at 6:30 a.m.; from negotiating for a bride, sight unseen, from a person's native land to negotiating the chores a person's children will complete when they stay with the divorced parent every other weekend; from getting a job to negotiating to get a better seat on an airplane; and from buying a home to buying golf gloves. Each opportunity has the potential to improve your life and your financial condition.

Sixth, the book helps you identify when a negotiation situation is present and how to take advantage of the situation. It helps you understand all of the available options when faced with a conflict situation and reviews the process of negotiation. Finally, you will be able to determine what a negotiation is and what is it is not.

Seventh, I will prove that it is OK to ask and if the answer is no, that is also OK. During the last forty-plus years that I have been negotiating and teaching negotiations, I've met tens of thousands of people. Many are afraid to ask for something because they might be told no. When I teach a negotiation course, I suggest to the class that I have been told no more than everyone in the class put together, because I ask all the time. (And I am told yes most of the time.)

Eighth, I discuss how important ethics are in the negotiation process and show how positive ethics will significantly increase the probability of positive results.

Ninth, this book will improve your skill in asking and answering questions, especially in negotiation situations. Since most of our day-to-day negotiations include only a few issues, the skill of asking and answering questions is a key to success. How many of these questions have you ever asked or answered? How many have been asked of you?

Why are you so upset?
Is that the best you can do?
Haven't I always tried to do the best for you?
When will you get done?
I've done this many times; do you really want to show me?
I assume you will be home on time.
What have you left out?
What is your best price?
What are the other items that we can agree to?

Can't we talk about this later?
You will behave, won't you?
Why did you fail?
Does this look good on me?
Why do you think you deserve it?
When will it be delivered?
When will it be fixed?

If you have previously used any of these questions, you will thoroughly enjoy this book. If you have used five, then you certainly need this book. If you have used eight or more, you must read this book. This book covers several areas including the types of questions, how to ask questions, when to answer, and how to answer your opponent's questions.

Tenth, I aim to improve the results of the reader's telephone negotiations. The chapter on how to successfully negotiate on the phone provides key information. Each year it seems that we have more phone negotiations as we shop more from our homes and try to solve problems from our homes or businesses.

Eleventh, the book will improve your Internet and written negotiations. A dramatic change in the twenty-first century is the significantly increased use of the Internet for both business and personal negotiations.

Finally, I review how to maintain the negotiated agreement. When we negotiate, we set the ground rules for a future relationship. The key is to win the relationship, not just the negotiation. Too many "experts" teach people how to beat their opponent at the negotiation table. These experts never worry about nor do they address the relationship.

In summary, this is the first book that reviews the dramatic change in the negotiation process and provides the information we all need to know to be successful in (win) all of our negotiations in the twenty-first century and, even more important, to be successful in all our future relationships.

Note that throughout the book, I identify a series of specific Keys to Success that apply not only to day-to-day negotiations but also to every negotiation situation. These are proven and will help you to be significantly more successful. In the appendix, each Key to Success is listed again. This is both a review and a place to find these keys quickly to prepare for all future negotiations.

I
Achieving Success in the Twenty-first Century

CHAPTER 1

Negotiation in the Twenty-first Century

The model for negotiations in the twenty-first century will be significantly different than the twentieth century model. This is true for both the way in which the negotiation will be conducted and the major objectives of the negotiators involved in the negotiation. The significant change from an adversarial process to a compromise process is becoming more and more accepted each day. The purpose of this change is to improve the success rate of all future negotiations. There is little doubt that many negotiations in the twentieth century were failures based on the outcome of the negotiated relationship. This dramatic change has affected the way professional negotiators act in current negotiations and it has affected the way the process is taught, especially in company-sponsored negotiation seminars.

For many years, authors and teachers focused on the negotiation table and how to win at the table. This was their measure of success. History has proven that their focus was wrong. The true test of the success of a negotiation is the results of the relationship formed as a result of the negotiation. The purpose of the negotiation process is to set the ground rules for a future relationship. After we have agreement, we have a relationship for some time period. The true test is, was the relationship a win-win relationship? To understand why this change in focus is so important and so dramatic, we must first look at the negotiation process in the nineteenth and twentieth centuries in two key areas of negotiation: *labor-management* and *buyer-seller*.

The negotiation that first comes to mind for most people is the labor-management negotiation. Most families in the United States and the rest of the world are affected by labor-management negotiations. They impact each family's income and standard of living. Labor unions first appeared in the United States during the Revolutionary War and were somewhat active during the mid-1800s. These craft unions represented specific skilled workers with the objective of promoting the welfare of the skilled people that made up the union. Negotiations during this period mainly concerned a single issue such as pay. Once the issue was settled, union activity was generally very quiet.

During this period, unions had little leverage, due to a court ruling in 1806. When the Federal Society of Journeymen Cordwainers (shoemakers) struck for better pay after negotiations failed, the court ruled in favor of their employers. In the court's opinion, the common-law conspiracy doctrine (the principle that the interests of the public are harmed when two or more individuals conspire to do something as a joint action) applied to this strike. The court stated that unions were illegal combinations in restraint of trade. Because of this ruling, unions found it difficult to be a major force in the workplace for several decades.

Union leverage started to change in 1842 when the Massachusetts Supreme Court ruled in favor of the Journeymen Bootmakers Society of Boston. The Bootmakers refused to work for a company that hired nonunion labor. The court stated that the union's refusal to work was not illegal nor was it an attempt to persuaded nonunion people to join the union. (It effectively did force these people to join a union to be able to work.)

A key event in the history of labor-management negotiations occurred in 1869 in the United States with the formation of the Knights of Labor, the first national labor union and the first attempt to organize all workers. Before this time, most unions were very local in nature and were involved in only local issues. The new union expanded beyond its historical local craft base. For the rest of the nineteenth century and into the late twentieth century, the labor-management arena was filled with major strikes. Many times these strikes became violent, especially when companies hired strikebreakers so the companies could continue to produce their products. When there were negotiations, the only objective of the negotiators was to win at the table. Winning at that time meant that one side had to lose, so at the start of almost every negotiation the expectation and the objective was for a win-lose outcome. Many books have chronicled the violence on the picket lines. Some of the worst examples were in the coal mines and steel mills in Pennsylvania and West Virginia. Thousands of people were killed, many more were injured, and even more families were destroyed because of the violence. This was true for both the union members and the strikebreakers.

During the 1950s and 1960s, major strikes disrupted the lives of almost every person in the United States. Four areas, the steel industry, the auto industry, the electrical industry, and the mines were often hit with strikes that created big win-lose contracts. The large unions implemented an important strategy. They would target one company in an industry to strike. (For example, in the electrical industry, the union would target Westinghouse. The union would continue to work at other major companies, such as General Electric.) This was a win-lose tactic, as it put a lot of pressure on the company that was struck. The companies' competitors were working and making bigger profits because supply was much smaller and, even more important, the companies that were still working were taking customers away from the company on strike. The company on strike was forced to settle on the terms that the union wanted. In all cases, this was a win-lose contract. After the contract was signed, the union went to all of the other companies in that industry and took the position that if the new contract was not matched, there would be more strikes. The objective for union negotiators was a win-lose outcome. During this period, in every new contract the unions won higher wages, significantly better benefits, and reduced workloads through prolonged strikes and negotiations that forced major concessions. These much improved benefits meant higher costs, so prices were raised almost immediately after the contract was signed. When costs went up, the cost of all products that used that industry's product also went up.

A 1959 steel strike that lasted 120 days almost shut down American industry, since almost all products made in the United States, at that time, used a significant amount of steel. Many workers in other industries were out of work because their companies could not get any steel. Profits and wages were cut, and it took many years before the impact of the strike ended. The steel union won most of their objectives, but the country paid a big price.

The aftereffects of this strike directly affected me during the 1960s. I was working in purchasing (buyer, supervisor, and materials manager) at the Small Motor Division of the Westinghouse Electric Corporation in Lima, OH. The contract signed after the 1959 steel industry strike was for three years (standard for that time). So every three years, I was tasked by my division manager (and by his boss the group vice president) with the objective, "Don't run out of steel." The objective was to have at least six months' supply on hand when the steel contract expired. To accomplish this objective in 1962 (the first time), we implemented a strategy to stockpile steel. Starting about nine months before the contract expiration date, we ordered almost twice as much steel as we needed each month. We had steel all over our factories, since the storerooms were not large enough to hold all our steel. The productivity of the four plants in this division was significantly reduced. There was no strike. So for the next several months, we were using steel from our inventory and the steel companies had very few orders.

In 1965 (the second time), I was tasked with two objectives: "Don't run out of steel and don't put any extra steel in the factories." To accomplish this added objective, we rented a large warehouse space (at a significant cost) and purchased an extra six months' supply of steel (again at a significant cost) starting nine months before the end of the next steel-workers' contract. Since during these times there was a high (false) demand for steel, the price of steel was also very high. Besides the large direct costs, there were indirect costs in the people area as my employees were working on strike risk containment instead of cost or quality improvements.

In 1968 (the third time), we decided to solve two problems, the extra cost for steel and the additional cost for warehousing, by purchasing foreign steel. The price of the steel was lower than U.S. prices and the foreign companies would ship during any strike period. This foreign steel proved to meet and for some requirements exceed our quality requirements. Again there wasn't a strike in the steel industry, but foreign companies had their foot in the door and continued to be a significant part of our steel-buying policy.

These win-lose steel negotiations, most people in both the business and the academic worlds agree, are one of the major reasons that in December 2001 twenty-seven steelmakers were under Chapter 11 bankruptcy protection, including Bethlehem Steel, the third largest steel company in the United States. In addition, hundreds of thousands (possibly millions) of steelworkers were out of jobs. Retirees were significantly impacted when many lost their pensions and medical benefits. I believe that the win-lose negotiations of the 1950s and 1960s became lose-lose relationships in the 1990s and 2000s. I believe that if both sides wanted a win-win relationship, most of today's problems would not exist.

The second major area of negotiations is buyer-seller negotiations. In the early years of industry, the owners generally purchased all the items for their company. During the late 1800s, as products became more technical in nature (as in the electrical industry), the chief engineer often would make important purchasing decisions. In the early part of the twentieth century, companies grew larger and the assembly line became the standard way to produce products. With more mass production, there was a need for more standard parts purchased in large quantities by a person with significant knowledge of the marketplace. Neither the owners nor the chief engineer had the time to do this, so a new position was created in most companies, the purchasing agent.

Another factor was the enactment of the first major antitrust laws (the Sherman Antitrust Act of 1890 and the Clayton Act of 1914) and the enactment of other laws (especially agency laws) regulating how businesses could handle their financial affairs. To address these needs, this new position developed in industry: the purchasing agent. In general, this person did not have a technical background, so the purchasing agent's major thrust in buyer-seller negotiations was price. The agent was expected to get the lowest price. With outside purchases being up to 30 to 60 percent of gross sales billed, all savings on purchased items went straight to the bottom line. Since price negotiations are really a zero-sum negotiation, these buyer-seller negotiations also became win-lose negotiations.

During my time at Lima, I was told several times by top management that my job was "to get the last penny out of every supplier." In discussions with other purchasing agents, both inside Westinghouse and at many National Association of Purchasing Agents meetings, I found that this "last penny" directive was a common objective. Management continued to see the purchasing department as the function that only considered price. Many purchasing offices had wall charts that showed cost (price) reduction objectives and actual reductions on a monthly basis. At that time, the concept of the five rights of purchasing (right quality, right quantity, right time, right supplier, and right price) was unknown to many people in industry.

This win-lose attitude between buyers and sellers in the United States was an important factor that opened the door for international suppliers when they came to the United States in the 1960s, 1970s, and 1980s. After World War II, products made in international factories were very low in quality. The price was also very low, but that did not offset the quality. Buyers knew they would waste their time if they investigated materials made offshore. During my time at the Westinghouse plant in Lima, I was approached by a French steel company that would be working during the time of a potential strike in the late 1960s in the United States. I gave this company a trial order. The steel we received was much better than the U.S. steel we were purchasing at that time. The steel was produced at a new mill that had been built after WWII. The steel mill used state of the art manufacturing techniques, such as basic oxygen furnaces, that produced steel that exceeded many USA specifications. We decided, with full approval from top management, to include this French company as a regular supplier to our division and as a result reduced our purchases from local suppliers.

In summary, during this entire period the objective of almost all business negotiations was to win at all costs. The results of these business negotiations were that one side was a winner and one side was a loser. Often there were bad feelings on both sides of the table. In many cases, due to normal human behavior, these win-lose negotiations became lose-lose relationships, as the loser at the negotiation table was determined to get even during the contract period. Changes in the process, the attitudes, and the objectives of negotiation were not seen until late in the twentieth century.

THE NEGOTIATIONS MODEL FOR
THE TWENTY-FIRST CENTURY

In the past twenty or so years, four truths have become accepted as keys to the negotiation process. As global competition has become significantly more intense, companies, unions, and others in the negotiation arena have been forced to examine the costs of the win-lose model of the negotiation process. These truths are as follows:

1. The purpose of negotiations is to set the ground rules for a future relationship.
2. The objective of negotiations is to find a win-win outcome.

3. The reason for negotiations is to satisfy needs on both sides of the negotiation table.
4. Negotiators must be evaluated by the results of the relationships formed by the negotiation, not just the negotiation.

A detailed examination of these four truths will demonstrate the seismic change in the negotiation process as we enter the twenty-first century.

The purpose of negotiations is to set the ground rules for a future relationship. At the start of every one of my negotiation courses, at the graduate or undergraduate level in college or at an in-company workshop, I state, "If you are here in this class/workshop to learn how to win at the negotiation table, you will be very disappointed and should leave now. In this class, you will not learn how to win a negotiation. You will learn how to win in your future relationships." Almost every negotiation is the start of a future relationship. When a buyer negotiates with a seller, the purpose of the negotiation is to establish a contract for the seller to ship the seller's product to the buyer's company. Key elements of the contract are price, delivery, quality, and payment to the seller's company.

When a union negotiating committee sits down with management, the purpose is to establish a labor contract that will cover the next three or four years of the lives of workers, managers, and customers. The working rules, pay, benefits, and retirement sections of the contract will have significant impacts on the profit of the company, the quality of life for the workers, and the cost to the customer of the product. After almost every negotiation, there is a relationship between the two sides. It may be for a few hours, a few days, a few months, or years. The relationship is the key.

The objective of negotiations is to find a win-win outcome. Since the two sides are going to live together for a period of time, they must find a win-win outcome. If not, the losing side will want to get even. When a negotiation ends, one of the first things that a negotiator does is to report to his or her boss or principal the results of the negotiation. If the negotiator says that he or she lost, the principal may make one of two statements: first, "You are fired," or second, "How are you going to get even?" It is very easy to get even during the relationship. My first example is a buyer-seller negotiation. If the seller believes he lost the negotiation, the seller can get even by shipping late, by shipping the lowest level of quality if there are several acceptable levels of quality, by shipping in small lots, by refusing to expedite shipments, or in many other ways. If the buyer believes he lost the negotiation, the buyer can get even by ordering in uneconomic lots, by spreading the order over several months, by closely inspecting each delivery for defects, by withholding payment of invoices or paying them late, or in many other ways. A win-lose buyer-seller negotiation can easily become a lose-lose relationship.

The same is true for labor-management negotiations. If the union believes it lost the negotiation, it can get even by refusing to work overtime, by only doing the minimum amount of work, by filing nuisance grievances, by actually destroying the company's products, or in several other ways. If management believes it lost the negotiation, it can get even by outsourcing items currently made inside the company, by building a new plant in a nonunion environment or even in an offshore location, or in many other ways. It is a fact that in every win-lose labor-management negotiation, the loser can get even. Win-lose negotiations will end up as lose-lose relationships. Today we cannot afford any lose-lose relationships.

The reason for negotiations is to satisfy needs on both sides of the negotiation table. Very few people ever negotiate just for fun. People only negotiate because they need something. Negotiation provides an opportunity to satisfy needs. This is a key to negotiation in the twenty-first century. The only reason industrial buyers put up with sellers is because the buyers need materials for their company. The only reason sellers put up with buyers is without sales their company will go broke. Why do union representatives negotiate with management? Because their members need jobs. Why does management spend hours negotiating with the union? Because management needs workers to manufacture its products. The results of survey after survey prove that the largest majority of people in the United States hate to buy cars because a difficult negotiation may be involved. People only negotiate because they have to negotiate, not because they want to negotiate. When one side (A) has something that the other side (B) needs, and B also has something that A needs, we have a great opportunity for a win-win outcome. Too many people, especially in the past, have overlooked this concept. Many negotiation books tell people how to win at the negotiation table. These books teach strategies and tactics intended to defeat the opposition. I have a lot of problems with these books, as do many experts in the negotiation field, in both the industrial and the academic worlds. It seems to be against all common sense to act in a counterproductive way when a person is trying to satisfy his or her own needs.

Negotiators must be evaluated by the results of the relationship formed by the negotiation, not just the negotiation. In the past, negotiators were evaluated soon after the negotiation was completed. Many times the evaluation was done the same day. The negotiator did a great job, a good job, a poor job, or a bad job. The evaluation was based on what was won and lost at the table. In large organizations, it was possible that other people would implement and manage the contract or agreement. They would be evaluated by the results of the contract, and the persons who negotiated it would be forgotten.

These four truths form the model for negotiations in the twenty-first century. Basically, future negotiators must focus on creating winning relationships by successfully completing win-win negotiations that satisfy needs on both sides of the negotiation. When this model becomes the norm, all relationships will be much better.

EXAMPLES OF THE NEW NEGOTIATIONS MODEL

A few examples are important for the reader's understanding of the change in the negotiation model. One example of the change in attitude about labor-management relations occurred in 1980 when, as part of the Chrysler bailout, Chrysler agreed to have the president of the United Autoworkers, Douglas Fraser, become a member of the Chrysler board of directors. Fraser became the first labor official to sit on the board of directors of an important U.S. corporation. A very interesting follow-up occurred in 1988. At that time Lee Iacocca, chair of Chrysler, was being pushed to run for the democratic nomination for president of the United States. Iacocca was asked to name his dream cabinet. He reviewed several potential appointments and then said, "former United Autoworkers President Douglas Fraser for [Secretary of] Labor or even better Fraser as the chief trade negotiator. He knows how to negotiate—take my word for it."A very short side bar in a spring issue of USA *Today* revealed this data. This I believe is the ultimate in respect and demonstrates a major change in labor-management attitudes.

A second example of a change of attitude in labor-management negotiations is found in the textbook *Business*, Fifth Edition, written by Ricky W. Griffin and Ronald J. Ebert:

> According to Edgar L. Bell, a former official with the United
> Steelworkers, the (new) system at LTV is promising because it has largely

moved beyond the long-standing premise of management-labor relations: "I had thought for a long time," says Bell, "that the way we conducted relations was crazy.... We are set up by law to fight. We had to fight to get the union, and then we had to fight to get a contract. Labor laws just set the rules for fighting."[1]

Jack Parton, a steelworkers' negotiator who worked on contracts at both Inland (Steel Corporation) and LTV, agrees: "We ain't going to survive by fighting every three years," he concedes. LTV chief executive David H. Hoag also sounds a conciliatory note: "There's definitely a place in American society for unions," he admits.[2]

A driving force toward a new negotiations attitude started in the 1970s when the Japanese were killing the U.S. steel industry with both quality and price. To survive, both labor and management needed to be more flexible. At some companies, this change came too late. For others, there is hope for the future. Employers have learned that positive employee relationships are a key to success and have come to understand the high costs of frequent turnover and poor employee morale. The new model for employee relations is involvement and empowerment.

As companies in the last twenty to twenty-five years have gone to producing products only in areas of their core competence, they have become significantly less vertically integrated. The result is that these companies are more dependent on outside sources for their production requirements. An attitude of win-lose with these sources means the end of the business. The objective of purchasing departments has changed from just low-price buying to completely managing all areas of the procurement decision. This has expanded to the concept of supply-chain management in the twenty-first century. Today, when purchasing people negotiate, they are expected to negotiate the total package, not just the price.

Examples of this changed attitude are found in the textbook *Purchasing and Supply Management* (Eleventh Edition) by Michiel R. Leenders and Harold E. Fearon:

> Negotiation is an attempt to find an agreement which allows both parties to realize their objectives....
>
> Negotiating a fair price should not be confused with price haggling. Purchasing managers generally frown on haggling, and properly so, for in the long run the cost to the buyer far outweighs any temporary advantage....

All negotiation has an economic as well as a psychological dimension. It is important to satisfy both of these dimensions to achieve a win-win result.[3]

CONCLUSION

This chapter has addressed the history of negotiation and how the model for negotiation in the twenty-first century has changed. The old negotiation model is no longer effective. The twenty-first-century world (both business and personal) will be the most competitive that we have ever seen. Every win-lose negotiation will create a lose-lose relationship, impacting the life of the organization or the family. The adversarial negotiation relationships of the past are no longer valid today, because these relationships cannot lead to a win-win outcome. The world and the United States have dramatically changed. We must evaluate future negotiators after the contract is completed, not when the negotiation is completed. The focus of negotiators in the twenty-first century must be on these keys: first, we negotiate to set the ground rules for a future relationship; second, we agree that the objective of negotiations is to find a win-win outcome; and third, we understand that the reason for negotiations is to satisfy needs on both sides of the negotiation table.

In professional sports, when a trade of players is completed, we are advised to wait a few years before we evaluate the trade. "Don't jump to a conclusion," we are told. "Just wait a while." This attitude is important for sports, but it is critical for all negotiations. I urge you to help establish a new negotiation measurement system in your company that will evaluate relationships, not just what happened at the table. I urge you to establish the same type of measurement system for all your personal negotiations.

Finally, it is important to understand that negotiation is not limited to just the business world and each of us is involved in many personal negotiations in our day-to-day lives. Almost everything in life involves negotiation, and negotiation is a key to success in our personal lives. The four key concepts of twenty-first-century negotiations must also apply to the important negotiations in our personal lives, such as husband-wife, parent-child, brother-brother, sister-sister, neighbor-neighbor, etc. Many of these personal negotiations are family negotiations and they must have win-win outcomes or the family may be divided forever. Most of us feel our family is the most important part of our life. How could we ever consider a win-lose outcome for even one family negotiation?

This change in the objectives of negotiation and the process of negotiation must be fully incorporated into all aspects of life as we face a shrinking world in the twenty-first century. The future success of our business, our personal lives, and our culture is directly related to how well we incorporate the new negotiation model into our daily lives.

CHAPTER 2

Winning Concepts

To be successful in all our negotiations, especially our everyday negotiations, there are seven key negotiation concepts that we must understand and use:

1. Win relationships
2. Satisfy needs
3. Buy now
4. Ask for
5. Perception versus reality
6. Self-fulfilling prophecy
7. Propose last

This chapter reviews these concepts in significant depth and provides examples from everyday negotiations.

CONCEPT 1: WIN RELATIONSHIPS

This is the first of two key ideas that are at the heart of every negotiation. The first idea is that we negotiate to set the ground rules for a future relationship. The second idea is that we negotiate to satisfy our needs. This concept is discussed next.

We negotiate to set the ground rules for a future relationship. Too many negotiators are very shortsighted. They want to win the negotiation and get the best of their opponent. This negotiation viewpoint is reinforced in many books on the subject. These books teach the reader how to win at the table. They give many strategies and tactics that will help the reader take advantage of the opponent. They put great emphasis on how to get power or leverage and how to take advantage of this power. It is my very strong belief that there are too many books with these ideas on the market and these books are being used much too often for advice and instructions. Most of the advice and many of the instructions are leading the readers in the wrong direction, away from success.

My basic belief is that we do not negotiate to win the negotiation. We negotiate to set the ground rules for a future relationship. Therefore, we negotiate to win relationships.

Does this concept seem strange to you? Is it heresy? How can a book about negotiation say "don't win the negotiation"?

Think about this for a few minutes. What happens after a negotiation has been completed? Typically, the two sides have to live with each other for the life of the contract or agreement. What happens if one side believes that they lost the negotiation? Many times that side may want to get even during the life of the agreement.

This concept is so important that we must briefly review what was discussed in chapter 1. When a negotiation between two organizations is over, the two negotiators (agents) are required to report back to their boss or principal. If one negotiator reports that he or she lost the negotiation, the boss usually says one of these two statements: (1) "You are fired," or (2) "How are you going to get even?" The fact is that both sides in the buyer-seller negotiation can get even. I do not want companies that I negotiated with working to get even with me during the life of our agreement. A second example is a management-labor negotiation. If labor or management believes that they lost, there are many ways to get even.

It is an absolute fact that in all business negotiations, if one side believes they lost (even if they did not really lose), they have many ways to get even. This attitude will make for lose-lose relationships and significant loss of profit for that business. In all of my future business relationships, I certainly don't want people trying to get even with me after the negotiation is completed. As I will review later in the book, this concept also holds true for personal and day-to-day negotiations.

Key to Success: Win Relationships, Not Negotiations

The get-even effect can also be seen in many of our personal negotiations. I believe that one of the reasons for the very high divorce rate in the United States is that one spouse always wants to win the negotiations (arguments), and does win, and the other spouse (the loser) gets even by first causing many problems and then finally by leaving. Each spouse must ask himself or herself, "Is this argument [small negotiation] worth risking the relationship?"

Consider parent-child interactions that are really negotiations. We all know parents can be very authoritative and always tell the child what to do and how to do it. They give the child orders from the time the child is in the crib until the child is a teenager. (Sometimes these parents give orders forever.) Every time there is a discussion, the parent's opinion prevails. Every time there is a disagreement, the parent wins the point. Every time there is a decision to be made (for example, where to go on vacation), the parent makes the decision. The child never wins. The child is never allowed to get his or her way occasionally or to have input into the family's decisions. The child has to put up with this environment because the child can't live on his own. The child will try to get even by doing exactly what the parent does not want the child to do. This is the child's way to get even while living under the same roof. Could this be a reason young people try drugs, get wild haircuts, drink, smoke, have unsafe sex, and don't do well in school?

But the real get-even comes when children are able to take care of themselves. Children leave home and never communicate with their family again. This is a real lose-lose relationship. The fact is that in personal negotiations, if either side believes that they lost, they have many ways to get even. In my personal life, I do not want people trying to get even with me. I expect that you don't want that in your life either.

It is most important always to remember that a completed negotiation can have three results:

- Win-win
- Win-lose
- Lose-lose

I define winning a negotiation as being able to obtain all or almost all of your objectives for that negotiation. It does not mean that your opponent has to lose. A major problem in our sports-centered society is that many believe that for me to win, you have to lose. This is true in games, but it is not true in negotiations. In a negotiation, if the other side gets all their objectives, that is great just as long as your side gets your objectives or most of them. In negotiations, you must not try to beat the other side; you must focus on obtaining your objectives. It is not possible to have both sides win a game, but it is possible, and must be our goal, to have both sides win the negotiation.

It is a fact that a large majority of win-lose negotiations become lose-lose relationships. Every outstanding negotiator can share examples where the negotiator left money on the table, so to speak, because the negotiator wanted a stable win-win relationship. I have hundreds of examples that can't be shared for confidentiality reasons. In these cases, I made a conscious decision to take less for the good of the relationship.

A fairly recent example of looking for a win-win relationship in my life is the fifteen-month period from June 1995 to September 1996. I was the lead negotiator for Advanced Micro Devices (AMD) in Sunnyvale, California, in a negotiation that led to a new company being formed to produce leading-edge photomasks to be used in the semiconductor industry. This was a four-way joint venture that included Micron Technologies (with a home office in Idaho), Motorola (main plant for this business in Texas), Advanced Micro Devices (two key plants in Texas and California), and Dupont Photomask Inc. (with the parent's headquarters in Delaware). Three of the partners (Micron, Motorola, and AMD) were the customers for and one (Dupont) was a major supplier of photomasks. The negotiation teams from each of the four partners usually consisted of several people, for example, two technical people (one from R&D, one from operations), a finance person, a legal person, a businessperson (generally buyer or seller), and an operations person. In several sessions, a person from corporate headquarters would be part of the negotiation.

The final component of this negotiation was that each partner had an internal principal. This was the person who most interested and had the largest stake in the negotiation. My principal was the chief scientist for AMD. As the negotiations progressed, every person had significant input into the process.

The process had two parts: formal negotiations and informal negotiations. We would meet on a regular basis (many times by video or phone). Between meetings, there were many phone calls and discussions about the issues to be negotiated. A key point for all involved was that every contact between the partners was a negotiation.

The result of these negotiations was that a new limited-liability cor-
poration (LLC) was formed and a new plant was built in Round Rock,
Texas. We expect that this new company (DPI Reticle Technology
Center) will be in business for many years.

It is a fact that the four partners will have to live with each other for
many years. Each lead negotiator had to keep this in mind at all times
during the formal and informal negotiations. It could have been possible
to win a few extra points during the negotiation, but lose a lot of issues
and money during the life of the LLC.

In summary, this is a key concept for success. Your objective must
always be to win relationships, not to win negotiations. I have found that
this is what separates professional negotiators from the many poor negotiators. There will be very few, if any, negotiations in your life that will
never require you to interact with the other side again.

CONCEPT 2: SATISFY NEEDS

Early in every seminar, class, or workshop that I teach on negotiations,
I ask one of the students, "Have you ever negotiated with me in the
past?" (Of course it is a person I have never seen before.) The student
looks perplexed and answers, "No, this is the first time we have ever seen
each other." Then I ask, "Why haven't we negotiated?" Again the student is perplexed. After several seconds I answer for the student: "Because
I did not have anything that you needed and you did not have anything
that I needed." Then I make the point that if that person did have
something I needed, I would have sought out that person and started a
negotiation to try and satisfy my need. If I could satisfy a need that person
had, the person would have looked for and found me in order to satisfy
their need.

We negotiate to satisfy our needs.

Think about this concept for a few minutes. Why do people or
companies negotiate? They negotiate to satisfy their needs. Why does an
industrial buyer negotiate with a seller? Because the buyer must buy a
product for his or her company. If the buyer does not buy this product,
the company will be in big trouble. Why does the seller negotiate with

the buyer? Because the seller's company must sell its products or else the company will fail. In this negotiation, both the buyer and seller are negotiating to satisfy the needs of their respective companies. Why do many buyers and sellers act like fools and try to take advantage of the other side? If either side, for example the buyer, pushes too hard and demands a very unfair deal then their opponent, the seller, may back out, and the buyer will not get the products the buyer's company needs. I have never understood why so few negotiators really understand the concept that we negotiate to satisfy our needs. I can never understand why so many people act like fools and do not conduct themselves as professionals during negotiations. They are really hurting themselves, sometimes more than they hurt the other side. We negotiate to fulfill our needs. This is true in our business and our personal lives. Do you know anyone who goes out on a Saturday morning to negotiate with a car dealer just to negotiate, with no intention to buy a car? In our busy lives, we do not have the time.

Key to Success: Professional Behavior Gets Positive Results

It cannot be stressed too strongly that people who act in a professional manner during negotiations will obtain the best results. Yelling, swearing, table pounding, and so on may gain a momentary advantage at the negotiation table. This advantage will be short and usually will turn out to be a big negative during the relationship. Personally, I have a major problem with some negotiation books that try to teach you to get every last penny out of every negotiation. These books only focus on the negotiation and completely forget the relationship.

Key to Success: Remember, You Negotiate to Satisfy Your Needs

In your personal life, why do you negotiate with anyone? Because that person can satisfy one of your needs. In my college classes I ask students to make a list of the negotiations they are most interested in learning more about in the class. I also ask for a list of the negotiations they most dislike. More than 90 percent state they hate to buy a car because they do not like to have to negotiate with car salespersons. Many students add that this is true for all of their friends. (Later in this book I hope to convince the reader that car buying can really be fun.) But they do negotiate. Why? Because they need a car. (Their car may be falling apart, or the family situation has changed, or they want to keep up with their friends, etc.) They feel that they need a car, so they negotiate. The car salesperson has a family, has bills to pay and other obligations, and therefore is more than willing to put up with the buyer to make a sale and earn the commission. Buyers have a need for an auto; sellers also have needs (both personal and for their company).

I very strongly urge you to be professional whenever you negotiate. First, it really is the right way to behave. Second, it will make for much more pleasant negotiations. Third, you want to satisfy your needs. Need satisfaction equals a happier and higher quality of life for you.

The photomask negotiation referred to earlier is a good example of this concept. Why did these four companies get together and negotiate a deal? Because each company had a major need. Dupont was planning an initial public offering and needed to increase its sales because it would become a separate company. AMD, Motorola, and Micron needed a way to ensure that they had the ability to purchase leading-edge photomasks in order to be more competitive in their individual markets. All four companies had significant needs and worked hard to satisfy their needs. In the process, each one satisfied the other companies' needs.

For success in all of your future negotiations, a key to success is to remember that you will always negotiate to satisfy your own needs. If the negotiation fails, you will be hurt (maybe even more than your opponent). It may seem selfish to say this, but it is true that you are negotiating to satisfy yourself.

Now that we understand that we negotiate to satisfy our needs, let us review a key to success in negotiations. Work hard, in every negotiation, to satisfy your opponent's needs first. This may seem to be 180 degrees from your objective, but do not stop reading. Please understand why I know that this is a key to success.

Key to Success: Satisfy Your Opponent's Needs First

What I try to do during the planning stage of every negotiation is to determine what I believe my opponent's objectives (needs) are in this negotiation. During the early stages of the negotiation, I work hard at confirming these objectives. I will do a lot of probing and questioning to try to get on the table the opponent's needs that must be satisfied to make an agreement. Next I try to develop situations in which the opponent's needs (or most of them) will be met. I confirm that if these things happen, the opponent will sign on the dotted line. Now I have the leverage in the negotiation. Why? Because my opponent's needs will not be satisfied unless there is an agreement or a contract. What will it take to have a contract? My needs must be satisfied. So now my opponent must work hard to satisfy my needs. If my needs are not satisfied, there will not be a contract (and the opponent's needs will not be met either).

The amateur negotiator goes into a negotiation stating, "I want this, I want that, I want, etc." The poor negotiator only considers his or her own side of the table and what the negotiator and the principal need. This usually will turn off the opponent. The professional negotiator goes into a negotiation asking, "What do you need to make a deal?" This usually turns on the opponent. The atmosphere in the room is much more positive. The professional has much more power and will be able later in the negotiation to satisfy his or her own needs.

Remember, you are never forced to sign the contract. If you do work out ways to satisfy your opposnent's needs and then the opponent fails to give you anything, you have the ability to walk away from the deal.

This key to success states that you want your opponent to work hard to satisfy your needs, and the best way for this to happen is if your opponent will be able to satisfy all or most of his or her needs when there is an agreement. There will be times when the needs conflict. Here compromise is a must. That is, your opponent wins one of the points in conflict and you win a second point if conflict. I've found than many times it is easier to have two issues on the table at once. This way both sides can obtain a win at the same time and keep a positive atmosphere at the negotiation table.

When people negotiate with each other, in families, businesses, other associations, or groups, they do so because they have needs. They also acquire things because they have needs. Sometimes they believe they need something but really don't, and this is called a want. It is very important for a negotiator to separate the needs from the wants. Your opponent may demand things that are really the opponent's wants (which you cannot satisfy), and if you can get to the needs (which you can satisfy), you will reach agreement. For example:

People want big cars and expensive homes.
People need quality transportation and shelter.

People want fame.
People need recognition.

People want to dominate.
People need to guide and influence.

People want prestige.
People need respect.

People want high salaries.
People need security.

People want long life.
People need good health.

Separating and understanding the difference between what people want and what they need is a very important key to negotiation success.

To summarize these first two concepts for success (win relationships and satisfy needs), here is an example from the life of Conrad Hilton.

Conrad Hilton built a billion-dollar hotel empire using the negotiation skills that he learned working in his father's dry goods store. Hilton's life has been compared many times to a roller-coaster, as he was close to bankruptcy on several occasions. During the late 1920s, his "empire" had grown to eight hotels in Texas, and he was in the process of building a major hotel in Dallas when the Great Depression started. Because he had a large debt load that he could not pay off, he lost all but one hotel. Therefore, during the early part of the Depression he had to negotiate with his suppliers to get them to give him money so that he could pay a

$40,000 lease payment on the only hotel he still owned. He asked seven suppliers (plus his mother) to give him $5,000 each to make the payment. He promised that he would always buy from these companies as long as he owned hotels. (This might be an early example of what in the 1990s we called supply chain management.) Why did these companies give him what today would be hundreds of thousands of dollars? They knew that his basic negotiation philosophy was this:

Be sure that the buyer gets a bargain and the seller gets a profit.

They knew that if Hilton got over his short-term problems, he would be successful. These suppliers wanted to be part of his success. They understood the risk, but they felt that the potential reward was so great that it was a good risk to take.

This is a great example of both concepts: win relationships and satisfy needs.

CONCEPT 3: BUY NOW

A major mistake that most people make when they are buying items for themselves is that they only buy when they have to buy and when they really, really need the item. When they buy under these circumstances, they lose a key leverage point in the negotiation—being able to walk away.

If a salesperson knows that you have to buy today, why should the salesperson negotiate? That person knows that he or she has a sale. This is especially true if there aren't many competitors nearby. It is also very true if you tell the salesperson that you want that product (by verbal or nonverbal communication).

Consider this example. Your refrigerator dies. It cannot be fixed. You call your neighbor on the right and ask if the neighbor can keep some of the food from your refrigerator for a few hours. The neighbor says yes, so you take all these items to the neighbor's house. Then you call the neighbor on the left and ask if that neighbor can keep the items from the freezer in her freezer for a few hours. The neighbor says yes, so you take all the freezer items to that neighbor's house.

Now you go to buy a new refrigerator. You look at a few models. A sales representative asks if he can help. Your first question is, "Do you have this model in stock and can you ship it today?" You have disclosed that you must have a refrigerator today. The real need is delivery today. You have lost all leverage in the negotiation. The sales representative knows that he does not have to cut the price to get the sale. The sales rep may even make more profit or commission by adding a delivery charge "to ensure delivery today," when normally delivery is free.

Key to Success: Buy When You Do Not Have to Buy

When an individual tries to negotiate with a big or small company, the company has most of the leverage. The need for that individual sale, to the company, is less than the person's need to buy. The best leverage an individual has is the ability to walk away. When the individual starts to walk out, the pressure shifts to the company. When the sales representative says, "Wait a minute. Don't walk out. Let's talk about this," the negotiation has really started and the individual has leverage and should get a better deal. Therefore, it is very smart to do a lot of shopping and reviewing sales and always be current with the prices of the items you will have to buy in the next couple of years.

I understand that many times we do not have the ability to buy later, nor do we have the money to buy early. But the more we can plan to do this, the better deals we will negotiate. Many families that I have worked with have an item in their personal budget titled "Purchases to be identified." This is money that they set aside to take advantage of opportunities in the future to negotiate a good deal for themselves.

CONCEPT 4: ASK FOR

You never get more than you ask for in a negotiation. Repeat after me: You never get more than you ask for in a negotiation.

Assume you are an industrial buyer talking to a seller. You want to buy 1,000 widgets. (Why do so many book examples use widgets?) The list price for one widget is $27. You decide to negotiate and make an offer to the salesperson to buy 1,000 at $23.95. (This is your initial position. Your objective is to buy at $25.) The salesperson agrees and shakes your hand. You are very pleased, but did you leave any money on the table?

The answer is yes. Very, very few times will the buyer's first offer be exactly at the seller's bottom price. The seller is happy to sell at any price above the seller's bottom line. The buyer will never know the bottom line unless the buyer asks for a price below the bottom line. The seller cannot agree to that, and after much negotiation the buyer raises the offer and reaches an agreement.

Key to Success: Start with Low Offers

If the first offer is accepted, the offer was a bad offer. Here are two examples, the first from the buyer's side. A friend's wife collects masks. She has them from all over the world (Alaska, India, China, South America, Africa, Southeast Asia, etc.). Our friend and her husband were in Bali looking at masks that were copies of masks from the Ramayana story. She found a "really great" mask and asked what the price was. The artist looked at the mask and said $125 US. My friend's wife quickly said, "All I have with me is $95." (She had read that it is a good tactic to say, "I would like to give you more, but this is all I have.") The artist said, "OK, the mask is yours." The wife was very pleased and even bragged to me about how she had saved $30. The fact is, she certainly paid too much. If the artist said yes that quickly, you know that the artist liked the price and didn't want the buyer to change her mind.

Here is an example from the seller's side. One of my students was getting married and decided that she would sell her condo, her future husband would sell his condo, and they would buy a house to live in. She had a real estate agent, but she set the price herself at $227,900. The first potential buyer agreed to her price and the condo was on the market for one day. During class, she shared how really happy she was to get her price and to sell the condo so quickly. It was so fast that she was going to have to store her stuff and live with her boyfriend. Before she had finished, many of the other students realized that she had made a bad deal and had lost money.

Here is another key to success: If you ask and you are told no, you have not lost anything. The agreement is at the original offer.

Key to Success: You Lose Nothing by Asking

I'll use the widget example again. The list price is $27. If you are the buyer, your job is to save money, so you start to negotiate.

You offer to buy at $22.50 and the seller says no.

Then you offer to buy at $23.25 and the seller says no.

Next you offer to buy at $24.95 and again the seller says no.

You raise your offer to buy to $25.75 and the seller still says no.

Finally you make your last offer at $26.60 and the seller says no.

Since you need the widgets, you agree to buy at $27 and a contract is made with the seller. Except for some time, you have lost nothing. The original price was $27 and you paid $27. You lost nothing by asking.

But you gave yourself the opportunity to save some money. The seller may have had an objective price of $26.50 and when you offered $26.60, the seller was happy to accept. This would be a great example of a win-win negotiation. The seller gets more than expected and the buyer pays less than expected. It is very important to remember that if you ask for something and the other side can agree right away, the other side must be very happy because they have realized more than they wanted. So it is important to be prepared for the next step. That is, you ask for more.

Using the above widget example, the list price is $27 and you as the buyer offer to buy at $25.95 and the seller says "sold." You know the price is too high, so you go to your backup and say, "Of course, based on the learning curve, that is only for the first 1,000 pieces. I will pay you $25.25 after the first 1,000 pieces." If the seller says OK, you know that the price is still too high and continue by saying, "Again, based on the learning curve, my $25.25 offer is only for the next 3,000 pieces. After I buy 4,000 total pieces, I will only pay $24.70." The seller might say, "That is not acceptable," and you agree on a price of $25 for the balance of the order. Having a next step is critical to your negotiation success.

Another example will summarize these two keys to success (Start with Low Offers and You Lose Nothing by Asking). Remember, if you ask for something and the other side can agree, the other side will be happy to give in. The other side has received more than its objective. I once asked a person who hitchhiked across the country during a summer break from college, "How could you just stand there and watch cars pass you by?

Especially when some may have made crude gestures at you?" The person replied, "Yes, I got told no a lot, but every day I got a ride. If you don't ask, you will never get." Then the person added, "I always asked them to take me a little further down the road than their cutoff point and you would be surprised at how many times they did drive more just to help me."

Key to Success: You Never Get More Than You Ask For

Why is this concept a problem for many people? Because people feel personally rejected if the other side says no. They feel it is better not to ask than to ask and be told no. What happens is that they leave a lot of money on the table. It is OK to be told no. A large percentage of the time, the no is not personal. The no is not against you as a person; it is against the position you are taking. Again, in the above example, if the buyer asks for a price of $22.50 (and the seller's bottom price is $25), when the seller says no it is because of economics, not because the seller dislikes the buyer. The seller would say no to anyone who asked for $22.50, even the president of your company or the mayor of your city.

Writers, lovers, negotiators, salespersons, and many businesspeople in general seem to have one thing in common: They must face a lot of rejection in the pursuit of their objectives. When a lover is rejected, the other person usually pulls his or her punches and makes it as easy as possible. For example, "I'm sorry, Diane, but our relationship just isn't going to work out. You are just too smart and too successful for someone like me." For writers, many times the rejection is a form letter that says the work is unacceptable, or worse. While it is true that the rejection is usually in a form letter that says something very vague like, "does not meet our needs at this time," the potential author takes this as a personal rejection of both the book and the author. The author can easily read between the lines. I read that George Orwell received a rejection for his eventually very successful book *Animal Farm* that said, "It is impossible to sell animal stories in the United States." I also read that the writer William Saroyan received 7,000 rejection slips before getting his first work published. By never giving in, he won the Pulitzer Prize in 1940. As an author, I have firsthand knowledge of receiving rejection notices. There were many for my first two books, but both books were published.

For negotiators, our positions will be rejected many times in a single negotiation. We will make many proposals, offers, and so on, and the other side will say no. This is not personal. But if you don't ask, you will never receive.

> **Key to Success:** Do Not Take a Rejection as a Personal Rejection
>
> **Key to Success:** Do Not Make a Rejection Feel Like a Personal Rejection

CONCEPT 5: PERCEPTION VERSUS REALITY

Many times, the perception of the negotiation is 180 degrees different on one side of the table than it is on the other. The story of two brothers who have an alcoholic mother is a good example. One brother drinks because he says he will become an alcoholic just like his mother, so he might just as well enjoy himself. The other brother does not drink because his mother was an alcoholic, but he enjoys himself just as much as his brother.

Another example is a father who is very strict with his two children. One grows up and is just as strict as the father because "It made me become a good person and I will make my kids become good people." The second is very easy with the children, has no rules, and so on, because "I don't want my kids to go through what I had to go through."

Each of us looks at the world differently. It is as if we had glasses on that filter what happens in the world before events get to our brain. An idea from the psychology world that we should understand is the Lewins lens concept. Lewins wrote:

- We see what we want to see.
- We hear what we want to hear.
- We accept what we want to accept.

This helps me understand many of the problems we have in the world. For example, the child next door gets in trouble at school and we may say, "Too bad his parents didn't bring him up right." Our child gets into the same type of trouble and we say, "The school is just out to get her." We see things differently depending upon what is in our "lens." How does this relate to negotiation? Each issue has value, and different people will see the value differently. For us to reach our objectives, we may have to help the other side understand the full value of our concessions. For example, a seller may offer to stock materials for a buyer. The seller knows that the cost will be high (17 percent per year) but wants to get the sale. The seller wants to get the sale at the list price. The buyer will never agree to buy at the list price until the buyer understands the true value of the stocking agreement.

In summary, in many negotiations a person is successful because the person helps the other side understand the value they are really getting instead of what they perceive they are getting. This is especially true when making a concession to them. If they don't believe that this is a major concession, they will not place a large value on the concession.

CONCEPT 6: SELF-FULFILLING PROPHECY

You have heard of the concept of a self-fulfilling prophecy. If I expect something to happen, it will generally come true. If I expect problems in a meeting, I'll look for problems and will find problems.

One of the joys of my life is playing golf with my son. When he was young, I could shoot a better score than he could. This did not last very long, and for many years he has beaten me every time we play—except for one hole on the Shoreline Golf Course near my home in Palo Alto, California. The fourth hole at the time we played was a short par three hole of about 165 yards. This distance is not a challenge even to average golfers. What makes the hole a challenge is that the golfer must hit the ball over water. I have seen many golf balls go for a swim in that lake (even a few of my own).

My son has never hit a ball over the water. It always goes into the lake. He "knows" that he cannot hit a ball over the water, and he doesn't.

My son has hit his ball with a 9 iron and it went into the water.

My son has hit his ball with a 7 iron and it went into the water.

My son has hit his ball with a 5 iron and it went into the water.

My son has hit his ball with a 2 iron and it went into the water.

One day my son took out his driver and said, "I don't care where this ball goes, but it will go over that water. He addressed the ball, swung, and hit the ball right into the middle of the water. He just knows that he cannot hit a ball over that water. It is a self-fulfilling prophecy.

On the next hole (number 5) after he hit his ball into the water with a driver, he took that same driver (and a new ball) and hit a perfect drive of 270 yards right down the middle of the fairway.

In negotiations, if I believe that I will do well, I will do well. My attitude going into the negotiation is a key to the outcome of that negotiation. Earlier in this book, I stated that many people do not like to buy cars. Why? Generally it is because they believe that they will not do well and will be taken advantage of by the salesperson. They are intimidated. They believe that the salesperson has more skills that they have. Many times this is not true.

In my second book, *The Human Side of Negotiations*, I review this formula for power (or leverage):

$$P = PI + PY$$

where

   P = power
   PI = the power I believe I have before the negotiation
   PY = the power you let me have during the negotiation

In this formula, PI can become your self-fulfilling prophecy, if you are not careful.

CONCEPT 7: PROPOSE LAST

It is always best not to make the first proposal. You should always get the other side to make the first proposal. You have everything to gain and nothing to lose. The proposal may be better than your objective and you get more. If it is not better than your objective, you just reject the proposal and start the negotiation.

I have thousands of examples of this concept, many from interview and hiring negotiations. One of my students in an evening negotiations course, was downsized and had a second interview scheduled that week with another company in the Silicon Valley. She had been making $57,000 a year. She really needed steady income starting as soon as possible, so she was prepared to take any salary over $50,000. We talked and she agreed that even though she really needed the job, she would control herself and not give a salary target. The interview went very well and finally the other person said, "We believe that you are a perfect fit for our needs. We want you to work for us and we are willing to start you at $62,000." My student was stunned. She just sat there. She could not speak. The other person took this as a no and said, "If that isn't high enough, we could go to $65,000." My student said OK and the deal was finalized. In the first year, she received $15,000 more salary, because she let the other side make the first proposal. Had the other side started at $45,000, my student had the opportunity to say no to that opening offer and to ask for more. My "commission" was dinner at a five-star restaurant.

Key to Success: Let the Other Side Make the First Proposal

Another example involves selling an older car. Always let the buyer make this first offer. A neighbor did this with a 1976 MGB and made $1,500 more than expected. The buyer really wanted that car and was willing to pay top dollar. My neighbor was, of course, willing to accept top dollar.

I could write a book with nothing but examples of situations in which letting the other side make the first offer was a major advantage in a negotiation. This concept is especially important in our day-to-day negotiations.

In summary, this chapter has reviewed seven key concepts for successful negotiations. These concepts will apply to every negotiation you are part of for the rest of your life, big or small, business or personal, and national or international. They are truly keys to success, especially in our day-to-day negotiations. We must continue to focus on these concepts:

First, we want to win relationships, not negotiations. Focus on the long range. It is significantly harder to do this in a negotiation, but it will be a major way to improve all aspects of your life. We all have a need to see our win right then and there in the negotiation room. It is harder to wait for a while to see that we in fact won, but if we do wait, then the win will be much better.

Second, we must remember that we are negotiating only because we have a need. Generally the other side also has a need, but it is our need that motivates us to negotiate. Always be professional and focus on satisfying your needs.

Third, whenever possible, buy when you want to buy, not when you must buy. One of the ways a person can gain leverage in a negotiation is to be able to walk away from the negotiation table. The labor leader George Meany said, "Never sit down at a negotiating table unless you are willing to walk away." It you must deal, you will always get a bad deal. Remember that the other side may very easily pick up your urgency and they will know that they do not have to make any concessions to get a deal.

Fourth, always ask for more than you expect. This will give you room to move in the negotiation. If you start at your objective, the negotiation will become a take it or leave it negotiation or one in which you lose. You never get more than you ask for in a negotiation and you usually get less than you ask for. Also remember that it is OK to be told no.

Fifth, be able to separate perception from reality and be able to help your opponent do the same. Your opponents will be much more ready to agree if they completely understand the real value they are receiving in the negotiation.

Sixth, be aware of the self-fulfilling prophecy concept. Be positive when you negotiate. Most people when they buy a car expect to lose the negotiation, and they do lose the negotiation. The people that expect to do well will get the better deal. Remember $P = PI + PY$.

Seventh, be a "nice" person and let the other side make the first proposal. You can accept that proposal if it is better than your objectives, or you can reject it if it is worse than your objectives. But you will never know if you go first. Many believe, and they are very wrong, that if you make the first proposal you control the negotiation. In fact, the side that makes the response is in full control. That side determines where the negotiation will go. That side also determines if the climate of the negotiation will be conflict or compromise.

These seven concepts are keys to your success. If you remember each one of them and use them when applicable, your future negotiations will be much more successful.

CHAPTER 3

The Power of Questions

"The power of the mind lies not in the ability to know, but in the ability to ask. Behind the problem, lies the answer." This quote from *The Heart of Philosophy* by Jacob Needleman, professor of philosophy at San Francisco State University, summarizes one of the reasons for this chapter. The second reason is that in the twenty-first century, negotiations must and will be more win-win oriented. In most win-lose negotiations, the negotiators tend to tell the other side what the negotiator wants or demands. In win-win negotiations there are fewer demands, more questions, and more discussion of needs.

In chapter 1, I reviewed the history of the negotiation process, how the process is changing, and how it will continue to evolve in the twenty-first century. In chapter 2, seven key concepts for success were reviewed. In this chapter, I discuss the significant concept that the power of questions will bring more success to savvy negotiators. The purpose is twofold: first, to reinforce the point that the side that asks the most questions will generally do best in the negotiation, and second, to show the many aspects of the use of questions in the negotiation process.

In the twentieth-century model of negotiations, the stated purpose was to win the negotiation, have the other side lose the negotiation, and to be ahead in the relationship. These negotiations started with one side giving the other side their list of demands. During the negotiation, the sides gave in slowly and felt bad when they did. The idea was to give in as little as possible. The negotiator who was able to give in only a small amount was the winner. Many times the negotiator went public (that is, bragged to the media, which then published the results) to show that the negotiator was the winner because the negotiator gave less than the other side.

Now we see more negotiations in which both sides work to develop a win-win relationship. More people understand that this is the key to success. They do not want to repeat history with negotiations ending with winners and losers (with the losers trying to get even), or both sides losing in the long run.

The first source of material for this chapter is the many hundreds of courses and seminars I've taught in several nations where I have watched and listened to students' complete case studies. Thousands of these business professionals, managers and executives, and nonbusiness people alike have lacked the basic ability to ask questions properly, to answer questions correctly, and to use good timing. Most of the time, people shoot from the hip in asking questions. The more skill we develop in asking and answering questions beforehand, the fewer problems we will have in the future. The savvy negotiator will give some thought to the purpose and function of questions and how questions can help us win all of our negotiations.

Another source of material was Hank Calero, who provided assistance when I wrote my second book, *The Human Side of Negotiations*. Hank also provided a lot of the raw data for this chapter and he wrote other books, including *How to Read a Person Like a Book*. After that book was released, the publisher organized a big promotional tour across the United Sates. Hank was interviewed by numerous newspaper, radio, and TV person-alities. During this period, Hank discovered most of these "professional" interviewers lacked the skill of asking questions and made two very common mistakes. Hank noticed they often asked a question and then answered it instead of being silent. The second mistake was asking too many yes-or-no-type questions. Almost every person who interviewed Hank made these two major mistakes.

Key to Success: Don't Answer Your Own Questions

The second mistake can be demonstrated when we think about how difficult it is for an interviewer (or a parent) to get information from a child with questions that can be answered yes or no. The child is happy with this type of question because the child does not want to volunteer information and get into trouble and the child is very happy to answer with just a yes or no.

Key to Success: Don't Ask Yes-or-No Questions

Another source of material was watching Sunday morning interview shows. One I specifically remember featured some of the nation's top reporters and journalists quizzing a prominent Washington, DC, lawmaker and a top cabinet official. This quickly became a very important laboratory for me as I listened to them inquire about a variety of subjects.

My first observation was how many times the person asking the question tended to make a judgment before the question was completed, with questions such as, "Isn't it true that . . .?" or "Why have you gone against public opinion on . . . " In almost every case, the answer was an evasive response or a conflict response because the person did not agree with the judgment. Either way the questioner lost power or information.

My second observation was how effective the questions were that did not make a value judgment, such as, "What's your position on gun control?" or "Do you plan to run for another term?"

My third observation was how often the person asking questions made a very lengthy statement, which in some cases was his or her position, before asking the question. Generally what followed the lengthy monologue was a simple question like, "Is that acceptable?" or "Do you agree?" It took a lot of concentration for the interviewee, who was on the hot seat, to listen carefully to what was being asked and to engage the mind sufficiently to answer quickly when the questioner finally stopped.

My fourth observation was that the most effective answers were simple answers, especially to complex problems. The least effective answers were very complex answers to simple questions.

My fifth observation was that good answers always put the most important information first in the answer.

A fourth major source of material was my notes from the many real negotiations that I've been involved in during the last forty-seven years. I have thousands of examples of good and bad questions asked during the negotiation process. This basic research covered many levels of negotiation skills and many different cultures. One of the common threads was that the side that asked the most questions generally did the best in the negotiation.

Key to Success: The Side That Asks the Most Questions Does Best

---

When one side asked a large number of questions, it put the other side on the defensive. It seemed they were defending themselves and trying to justify their answers. This was especially true when there were many questions in a row.

Key to Success: The Side That Answers the Most Questions Does Worst

---

Another key point was that the side asking questions was not giving up any information and the side answering questions was giving up information. Even in the extreme case where the answer was yes or no, many times there was a nonverbal communication that gave away a lot more information.

Key to Success: You Must Get Information and Commitment to Be Successful

---

To achieve your objectives in a negotiation, you must get information and then get commitment from the other side. These two objectives are best met and completed by asking questions. Generally, it takes much longer to answer a question than it does to ask a question. During the answering time, the side that is talking is not learning and the side that is listening is learning. An easy way to reinforce this point is this simple two-liner:

Listening = learning information
Speaking = sharing information

> **Key to Success:** The Side That Talks the Least Usually Does the Best

The best way to remember this point is to remember that: Whoever you believe your maker to be, your maker sent you a very strong message by giving you two ears and one mouth. To me this means that we should listen twice as much as we talk.

> **Key to Success:** Remember That We Have Two Ears and One Mouth

A final key point before I get into details concerns answering questions: most people agree that the person asking a question has the power in the negotiation while they are asking the question. But when the question is finished, the other person has an opportunity to gain power based upon the answer. Here is an example that Hank uses in his conflict resolution workshops.

A stay-at-home wife does all of the laundry for the family, including her husband's dress shirts. One day the husband wears a shirt that has too much starch in the collar. He comes home and starts yelling at his wife: "I had a terrible day at work because of you. I have a thinking job and how can I think with too much starch in my collar? How many times have I told you, 'Don't put too much starch in my collars?'" At this point in their negotiation, who has all the power? The husband who is yelling or the wife who is listening? It is the wife.

The wife now has the opportunity to take all the power because she has many possible answers, and the one she picks is critical. A few examples:

1. "Wait a minute, buddy, you are not the perfect husband. Last weekend you were suppose to cut the grass and you didn't."
2. "I did it. I put too much starch in your shirt, and I'm sorry, but over all these years haven't I been a good wife and mother? Our son graduated from the Air Force Academy and our daughter is a leader at church."
3. "OK."

Note that the response will determine the direction of the negotiation for several hours or even days. The first response will cause conflict, and there will probably be a long fight with many angry statements as the two people move away from each other. The second response is a compromise response and will cause them to move closer (maybe even a hug and kiss). The third response causes nothing.

Key to Success: You Have a Lot of Power When You Answer a Question

The person answering a question has the power to shift the level of the negotiation to either conflict or compromise, or maybe nothing. When we answer questions, we must be aware of our opportunity and use that opportunity to our advantage.

Key to Success: Before You Answer a Hard Question, Determine Whether You Want a Conflict or a Compromise

In all our negotiations, in business and day-to-day situations, questions and answers are one of the keys to success. Generally in the small negotiations there are not as many issues to be negotiated as in large business negotiations, but in both types the use of questions is very important for success. Human interaction is the key to which side wins.

This chapter follows an outline with eight sections:

1. Examples of bad questions and their results
2. Purpose and types of questions
3. Alternatives available when questions are asked
4. Answers that can cause major problems
5. How to improve asking and answering techniques
6. The five toughest questions
7. Other observations
8. Summary

First, I cover how *not* to use questions, so that I can build upward. I then review many types of questions, including the problem questions that we face and how to handle them. I look at alternatives to answering questions, how to defuse their power, and how to gain momentum in the negotiation. Toward the end of the chapter there are a few comments on how to improve your question asking and answering techniques. I discuss a study that I did as part of the research for this book. I asked hundreds of people, "What are the five toughest questions you have been asked?" Their answers were part of the input for the book and many are listed for your information and amusement.

EXAMPLES OF BAD QUESTIONS AND THEIR RESULTS

There are thousands of questions that are bad questions. I will only review a few in this section so that you will get a good feel for what is a bad question. This should significantly cut down the number of bad questions you ask in the future and the bad results that often follow a bad question.

The classic bad question is one the can be answered yes or no. I remember a child being interviewed on TV by an adult who asked a series of questions that could all be answered with a yes or no. After the final question was asked, the child thought for a minute and then said, "Yes, no, and yes." The adult interviewer was visibly shaken and said, "What do you mean?" The child answered, "You asked me three questions in a row and I gave you three answers to the three questions, in a row. I have answered all of your questions." I hope that the interviewer was much more careful how she asked questions in the future, especially to children. This is a great lesson for every reader. If the answer to a question is yes or no, it is generally a bad question and the person asking the question will have to ask more questions to get the information wanted in the first place.

> **Key to Success:** Very Bad Questions Can Be Answered Yes or No

Another example of bad questions is when we ask too many questions. This causes two problems. First, I find that some individuals don't use good judgment on when to end their series of questions. That is, they seek additional information, but are not satisfied to wait a while to get it. They want it all now. Apparently they don't know that many people like to use incremental disclosure, instead of spilling their guts, as a way of giving information to others. These people are most comfortable giving out information in small pieces. When they are pushed, they dig in and refuse to give any more information. It is best not to push these people. Let the information come out at a speed that the other person can handle. This is especially true in negotiation and conflict situations.

The savvy negotiator will have a certain amount of patience in asking questions that seek additional information. Take what you can get. Wait. Then take a little more. Wait. Then take more. Remember that most individuals prefer to disclose incrementally and not spill their guts, so give them an opportunity to do so. When we seek additional information, we always run the risk of asking too many questions in a row, which could irritate the other person. Or as an answer to our question, we could get a monologue that has nothing to do with what we asked (see below).

Key to Success: Be Patient When Asking Questions

Many people know that computers are programmed to store a lot of information and then to display it rapidly whenever the information is needed. Humans are not computers. Emotions are not involved in the retention and display process that governs a computer, whereas emotions are of paramount importance where people are concerned. When someone asks us to "display" our stored information, we often give it up at a slow, begrudging pace.

Key to Success: Understand Slow Human Responses

There are, of course, several exceptions, such as someone who not only answers all aspects of the question but continues with additional information that is totally unnecessary. These individuals are very rare, and many times they hurt their position. Another problem with people who spill their guts is trying to remember what it was that they answered first. This was the information that the person asking the question really wanted. We tend to remember the last statement that we heard, which is not the information that was asked for.

THE POWER OF QUESTIONS   43

Another example of a bad question is the last and not-needed question. This question generally does not solicit any new information that will help the questioner's position and it may provide a way for the other side to give more information. This extra question, by providing too much information, hurts the questioner's position. I lived in Waco, Texas, for three years while serving in the U.S. Air Force. There is a story from Fort Hood, near Waco, that many swear is true, but I believe that it is an urban myth. Whatever the case, it is a great example of an extra question that should not have been asked. This is the situation. There is a court case where one soldier (I'll use the name Jim) claims that a second soldier (Bob) bit his ear off during their fight. (This was long before the Mike Tyson boxing match in the late 1990s when an ear was really bitten, and had nothing to do with that fight.) There is a witness (Jeff). The defense attorney for Bob is asking Jeff questions.

ATTORNEY: Did you see the start of the alleged fight?
JEFF: No.
ATTORNEY: Did you see Bob bite Jim's ear?
JEFF: No.
ATTORNEY: Did you see Bob actually bite off any part of the ear?
JEFF: No.

The attorney is now in a great position, since there is no proof Bob did anything. But the attorney had to ask just one more question.

ATTORNEY: Then how can you be a witness in this case and support Jim's claim that Bob bit off a part of his ear?
JEFF: Because I saw Bob spit out the ear.

Key to Success: Know When to Stop Asking Questions

A bad question many times is the extra question that our ego wants to ask to claim "complete victory." If you have the information you need to support your position, shut up.

In summary, we can get into a large amount of trouble in negotiations when we ask bad questions. Unfortunately, many people just blurt out a question, before thinking about the question and the many possible answers. This cautious step will save the savvy negotiator many problems.

PURPOSE AND TYPES OF QUESTIONS

Too many people believe that the purpose of questions is to get information. The entire process would be very simple and would require very little expertise if that were so. However, the process is considerably more complicated than is normally perceived. When we ask a person a question, we could be performing any number of different functions. There are also as many multifunctional questions as there are single-purpose inquiries such as, "What time is it?"

Research completed by Hank Calero and myself has identified at least twenty-seven different types of questions. Some of the different types may seem very similar. My purpose in listing all of them is to show the subtle differences and to illustrate the wide range of questions. With the new emphasis on win-win relationships, knowledge of the various types of questions is important to the savvy negotiator. The more tools available to the negotiator, the higher the probability of success. Sometimes, depending on the condition and relationship, each question might also become multifunctional. Don't assume that a question is a question is a question.

Studying the different types of questions will greatly improve your skill in asking and answering questions. Once you completely understand the differences and how to use the differences to your advantage, you will be able to use the right type of question to get the information or action you need. Also, it is important to note that a question and its purpose may change depending upon the circumstances of the negotiation (business, college, family, etc.). Understanding the differences will give you an advantage in every future negotiation. That is the purpose of this chapter.

In this area, I will review many examples so you can better understand the wide range of questions. The questions are listed in random order. Do not read into the order any priority system. A limited number of examples for each type of question are given. Understand that the limiting factor is space, not examples. The basic reasons that we ask and the main purposes of questions are to:

1. Seek information, general or specific
2. Ridicule, put down, or criticize
3. Set up another person for the answer we want
4. Get others to sell, persuade, or convince us
5. Attempt to get commitments or promises
6. Identify specific needs
7. Display our intelligence
8. Test assumptions
9. Probe further, explore, and get additional information
10. Draw attention to yourself
11. Evade questions
12. Control the other's behavior
13. Allow others to use their insight
14. Get reassurance for ourselves
15. Discover specific feelings, emotions, or beliefs
16. Find areas of mutual agreement or compromise
17. Isolate areas of disagreement
18. Get the opponent's attention
19. Divide the opponent's team
20. Eliminate semantic traps or problems
21. Restate or clarify a position (yours or your opponent's)
22. Set a deadline for action or agreement
23. Get the opponent to agree to a premise
24. Make a point when you know the answer
25. Pave the way for a more important question
26. Sidestep a question without angering your opponent
27. Bring a discussion to a close

Seek Information, General or Specific

Examples:

How much does this cost?
Who will clean up this mess?
What is the vintage of this wine?
When will the golf match start?

Will you live with me?
Are you a Yankees fan?

The most obvious reason why a person asks a question is just to get information. For many people, this is the only type of question they use. The asker just wants a specific piece of information. For example: "What time does the train leave?" "When do we eat?" "When do you expect to get home?" "What was the final score of the game?" and so on. These questions in most cases get a simple answer, such as, "2 p.m.," "in fifteen minutes," "after 10 p.m.," and "we won 2-1." Although we ask for specific information, sometimes we get it and sometimes we receive vague responses such as "soon" or "late." These answers now require an additional question such as, "How soon?" or "How late?" As many readers can readily recall, such a follow-up inquiry sometimes leads to an unleashing of emotions which then leads to arguments and hostile words that both parties later regret. Perhaps afterward you realize that the question seeking information could have been asked in another, better way and gotten the specific information that you really wanted without a hassle.

The basis for all questions that ask for information are the six words taught to freshman journalism students that come from this poem:

I keep six honest serving men
They taught me all I knew
Their names are What and Why and When
and How and Where and Who.

When you ask a question that asks for specific information, you are sometimes more successful if you cushion that question by explaining why you are asking the question. For example, instead of asking, "Where is the airport?" in a city where you have never been before, try, "I'm a stranger in your city. Could you please tell me where the airport is located?" Instead of "When do we eat?" you might say, "I really like your cooking. When do we eat?" In both cases, one might still get a response like "soon" or "that way." But the attitude and atmosphere created are entirely different, and your chances of getting a complete answer are much better. A very common family example is this: "When do you expect to get home?" versus "Last week we were very worried about you when you didn't get home by midnight. When do you expect to get home tonight?"

My research has proven that questions that seek information seem to be much easier to answer when the person asking the question gives some information first. Perhaps this is because many of us take questions to be negative or an attack and respond the same way or become very defensive. For example, ask people where they purchased an article of clothing without first saying that you like the way it looks. You will observe that they answer as though they sense that you do not like the clothing they are wearing. They assume your next comment will be very negative and a put-down. A final example will prove this point. If you ask your spouse, "Where did you buy this steak?" the probable answer is "Why, what's wrong with it?" However if you say, "I really like this steak. Where did you buy it?," the reaction will be totally different. In summary, it is extremely important when we seek information to first give some information in order to put the other person at ease relative to our feelings toward them, their actions, or their possessions.

Another way to do this is to recap what you already know and then state what additional information you seek. Police investigators are very skilled in this form of questioning. For example, a police investigator might ask, "We already know that you were not there in the room when Ms. Smith was killed. We checked and found you were somewhere else. What is important for us to know and what we must ask is . . . ?" Such recapping can be very useful in getting your questions out and getting good, direct responses to them. An ordinary example is when you are calling to complain. Start with, "I know that this is not your fault [the person you are talking to], but it is a major problem for me and I need to know . . ." You will probably get a much better answer.

There are international and cultural variations to improve the way you ask questions in order to get information. In Europe it is significantly better to be polite when asking a question. Earlier I used as an example the question, "Where is the airport?" I improved that question to, "I'm a stranger in your city. Could you please tell me where the airport is located?" In Europe that would be changed to put more emphasis on *please*, so the question would be, "Please excuse me. I'm a stranger in your city. Could you tell me where the airport is located?" In England we should start with, "I'm sorry to bother you, but I'm a stranger in your city. Could you please tell me where the airport is located?"

There are many ways to reword questions to get a better answer. I remember a very special TV interview with a woman whose husband had been killed in an airplane crash at an altitude of 11,000 feet. The interview was about her climb to the crash site to deliver a bouquet of flowers and say good-bye to her deceased husband. She was not an athletic type who could readily make a very difficult climb. In fact, she was almost a fat person. However, one could quickly see that she had a lot of courage in the way she carried herself and especially the way she spoke. The interviewer asked her this outstanding question: "How many people tried to discourage you from making the climb?" (Note that the normal questions such as, "Were you discouraged by others from going on this climb?" or "No doubt you were told not to attempt this climb?" could be answered by a simple yes or no.) When the interviewer asked, "How many . . . " this required a specific answer and opened the way to a tremendous interview. The woman answered, "Actually, no one discouraged me. Instead I received a great deal of support." She continued to describe how her family and friends helped in organizing the trip and the details on how she trained to get her body in shape for the difficult climb over very hard terrain. The wording of that lead question made the interview an immediate success, and the questions and answers that followed only served to prove that point.

Each of us can be more successful in asking questions by rethinking them, before they are asked, to reword them in order to get specific information rather than just receiving a yes-or-no response. Hank Calero tells an interesting tale that occurred a few years ago during a visit to Bombay, India. His watch was not working properly and was losing time, so one morning he decided to get the watch fixed. He asked the hotel staff if a jeweler or watch repair shop was nearby and was given directions to a store three blocks from the hotel. He easily found the store, walked in, took off his watch, and said, "Can you fix my watch?" Without responding, the store owner took the watch, removed the cover on the back, and proceeded to lay out all the internal parts of the watch on the counter. My colleague was shocked and was waiting for an answer as he watched his very expensive watch being field stripped like an automatic weapon. After what seemed like an hour, the shop owner finally looked up from the watch and said one word: "Yes." Hank recalls a great sense of relief and a feeling of foolishness to have put himself into such a predicament and such a weak negotiating position. When he was relating this experience to me he said, "I guess that was not a very good negotiating situation for me to be in, was it?" With the watch open and in many parts, the shop owner had all the power and Hank would have to pay whatever price the shop owner asked to fix the watch.

Indeed, we learn two things from this example: (1) Don't open yourself up to anyone by asking a yes or no question; and (2) Do not wait too long to get an answer once you discover that you have asked a very bad question. Once you have any answer, you can proceed further and, based on what you hear, ask a much better follow-up question. My colleague still worries about what he would have done if the shop owner had said no and left his watch lying on the counter in many small pieces.

Many a parent remembers how annoyed she was when a child asked, "When are we going to get there?" on a trip regardless of how short the trip might have been. The child had more sense than to ask a poor question such as, "Will we get there soon?," which would be an opening for a possible yes-or-no answer. Instead the child wanted specific information about time in order for the child to make a value judgment as to whether it would be "soon" or not. Similarly, in other situations, children often just seem to know how to word their questions to get the information they want.

Using parent-and-child situations, we can learn a great deal about the right and wrong way to ask questions. Let's look at a typical parent-child interaction in which the child just asked the parent for something.

CHILD: Can I have a . . . ?
PARENT: Yes [or no].

If the response is yes, then the child will then want to know when or how soon, which requires another answer or series of questions and answers. If the response is no, then the child in all probability will ask why, forcing the parent to justify the answer. Next the child might say something like, "Well, Carol's parents let her have . . . " This then becomes a long guilt trip that is very unpleasant for both the parent and the child. In this situation (and whatever the parent's response), the child usually is very clever in forcing the parent to justify all of the answers. (Maybe this is why so many parents who can't come up with any good ideas on how to justify their position often simply say "because," or even worse, "because I said so."

What would be a better way to handle this situation? First, the child's question could include a strong reason why the child needed the item. For example, "Next week they are holding tryouts for the soccer team. Can I have a new pair of soccer shoes?" Or, "Since it is the beginning of the month, do you have enough money for me to buy soccer shoes for the team tryouts next week?" It is always better to give reasons for the question, "Can I have . . . ?"

Another way to handle the situation would be to help the child develop better questioning skills. It is my feeling that if parents can help their children learn how to negotiate early in life, the children will become far more successful in whatever they do. Thus if parents make their children "work" for everything they get, the children are not only more appreciative of what they receive, but also the children develop wonderful negotiation skills that will serve them well in their adult life. Remember the six key words that are taught in freshman journalism classes—Who, What, Where, Why, When, How. Very good questioning skills will help to make your life be more successful.

Using this approach the interaction might go as follows:

CHILD: Can I have a . . . ?
PARENT: Why do you think you need a . . . ?

Now the shoe is on the other foot and the child must justify his or her need. Big difference, isn't it? After doing this many times, the child will learn to ask better questions to get what the child needs. The real benefit from such questions is that the child is forced into becoming a better negotiator. Since things are not automatically given to them when they ask for them, they start to negotiate to get them and to develop great skills for doing so in the future.

Key to Success: Help the Other Person When You Give Your Answer

---

Another interesting observation that I have made is that when we seek information and ask a question, the other person many times makes a value judgment. We ask a question to get specific information in order for us to make the value judgment, but we word the question in such a way that the judgment is made for us by the other person. For example, a shopper at a supermarket asks the grocer, "Is this fresh?," which almost always receives the same answer: "Yes." (What else should we expect from the grocer?) Instead, we might ask, "When was this produce delivered to your store?" Then we can make our own value judgment as to whether the lettuce is considered fresh, because the judgment will be by our standards.

During a trip to Mexico City for a seminar, my friend Charlotte decided that a trip to the pyramids would be worthwhile before she left. So one sunny morning, she asked one of the hotel staff members if it was very far to the pyramids. The answer was no, so she walked out to the Avenida Reforma, hailed a cab, and told the driver, "Pyramids por favor." The cab took off in the normal heavy early morning traffic. For the next thirty minutes there was continuous stop-and-go driving as the cab tried to get through the congestion and out of the city. The meter was running, so Charlotte asked about the distance remaining and was told, "About sixty-five kilometers and it will take at least one hour more." This was a very costly lesson for her. Later we discussed the fact that a much better question would have been, "How far is it to the pyramids?" followed by, "How long will it take?" The answer would have been, "About eighty-five kilometers" and "More than two hours" and she could have decided if that was too far to take a taxi.

There are many other examples. Here are three from my recent airline flights. On the first, I overheard a passenger ask the flight attendant, "How's your coffee?" She quickly answered, "Swell." Later, after the passenger had the first drink, he remarked to his seatmate, "This is really lousy coffee." The passenger asked a question seeking information, but allowed the attendant to make a value judgment for him, which he later regretted.

On the second flight I heard someone ask, "Is your coffee fresh?" and the answer was, "Yes, ma'am, all of our coffee is always fresh." Now this was a better question because it asked for more specific information relative to where and when the coffee was made, but did not ask if it was good or bad. Later I heard the lady say, "This sure doesn't taste freshly brewed to me." (It was fresh, but it was not good.)

Then on the third flight, a passenger asked the attendant, "On a scale of one to ten, where do you rate your coffee?" She gave a magnificent answer: "As a confirmed coffee drinker, I've yet to drink a cup of coffee on any airline that is as good as one made at home." The woman asking the question settled for a glass of water. Three different individuals had asked three different questions on the same subject and all received different answers. (You should know that I had coffee on all three flights, and it was acceptable.)

When you ask for specific information with a question that can be answered with a yes or a no, the answer may be colored by the views of the person who gives the answer. These views could include opinions, judgments, values, and so on. So you have to be very careful how you ask and react to the answers of these types of questions.

Another point is not to expect individuals to give you a full confession. I'm sure that every Catholic priest shortly out of seminary soon learns this lesson. Take whatever is given, accept it, and get more information later. This is a very fundamental factor for the reader to become a successful negotiator. When we seek additional information, we should consider that people like to disclose in increments. We must work to get what we want since very few individuals gladly give up information, especially about themselves.

A final example of value judgments comes from police TV shows. How often does the police officer at a crime scene ask a witness, "Was the person that ran away tall?" A five-feet six-inch person will give a very different answer than a six-feet four-inch person. The correct question is, "How tall was the person that ran away?" Another very sensitive area for value judgments is weight. Many fights have started over what is considered fat and what is not considered fat.

Ridicule, Put Down, or Criticize

Examples:

Are you suggesting that I am stupid?
Have you taken leave of your senses?
Where in the world did you come up with that idea?
What did I do to deserve that response from you?
Have you ever seen a worse golf swing?
Who picked the cast for this display of nontalent?

The purpose of the second type of question is to ridicule, put down, or criticize. The results of asking this type of question can vary 180 degrees. You send a very clear message with this type of question. No doubt we all have at some time been the victim of someone who sought to ridicule or put us down. They did not try to accomplish this by making a demeaning statement; rather, they used a question. One example is, "Have you taken leave of your senses?" Another I've heard many times is, "Where in the world did you come up with that idea?" On the surface it seems like a simple question is being asked, but the real meaning is not a query but a negative statement. The first type of question and those that follow ask for information or action from the other person. This second type of question is very different from the first type in that these questions usually give information, and the information is generally negative.

The results of these negative questions cannot be predicted. Two examples will illustrate this point. I was playing golf early one morning at one of the greatest golf courses in the world, Ballybunion Old on the west coast of the Republic of Ireland. I was a single and the starter assigned me to play with three other Americans. (I would much rather have played with three locals.) They were on a prepaid golf tour and this was their first course in Ireland. They would be playing together for the next ten days. They decided to make a bet of $2 US per hole with the low score for each hole winning all the money. I declined to be part of the bet, since I could very easily be set up. The first two holes were tied, so more was riding on the third hole, which was a par three 217 yards long. The first man to tee off used a 2 iron. His shot was straight, but a little short of the green. The next man also used a 2 iron from the tee. His shot was also a little short of the green, to the right, and in a sand trap. The third man pulled a driver out of his bag to hit his tee shot. The first man turned to the second man and asked this question: "Isn't it true that only small boys and weak women need to use a driver on a short hole like this?" The second man replied, "Yes, and do you think that there is any difference?" Both were fast put-down questions. They were not asked directly of the third golfer, but were meant for him, and he both heard and understood the message. In this case, the put-down backfired as the third man quickly developed a higher resolve to do well. With his club he hit a great shot that not only was on the green but only four feet from the hole. He made a very easy birdie putt to win all the money. The others didn't even make par on the hole.

On the next tee that man teed off first, because he had the lowest score on the last hole. Before he hit his tee shot, he said, "Since I'm either a small boy or a weak woman, I'm sure that you will not turn down my offer to increase our bet. Are you afraid to play against a boy or a woman for $5 per hole?" Another example of a put-down question. The others were in no position to refuse, and the third man won almost all of the money that day. The first put-down questions had backfired. I enjoyed watching the whole drama unfold as I remembered the old Arnold Palmer expression, "It's not how, but how many in golf." I also enjoyed it because the whole world is my research lab and I took notes for future negotiation classes.

This is a very good example of how the results of put-down questions are not always predictable and may be very unexpected. The results may end up negative or positive and in the above story both occurred. The first two men had a very bad result and the third man had a very positive result.

A second example comes from football lore, and the result was completely positive. One of the historic stories (maybe a myth?) of Notre Dame football is the one about Knute Rockne and a short half-time pep talk that he gave to his football team. Notre Dame was losing very badly that day and the first half of the game was filled with mistakes by the Notre Dame team. There were fumbles, missed assignments, missed tackles, and just overall very poor play. Their opponent was playing well, gaining confidence, and based upon the first half the opponent might have been able to pull an upset. The first half ended and the players headed for their locker rooms. The Notre Dame players were going very slowly as they knew once they got into the locker room the coach would really chew them out for their terrible playing during the first half. They had played poorly and deserved a good chewing out, but they knew that the less time they spent in the locker room, the less chewing out they would receive. The coach was well known for these types of anger communications and had chewed them out many times in the past.

After all the players, assistant coaches, assistants, and so on were in the room, the door was closed. They waited but after looking around discovered that Coach Rockne wasn't in the room. No one dared to say a word and the room was very silent. Everyone waited. Five minutes went by. Eight minutes went by. Ten minutes went by. Fifteen minutes went by and nothing. The team was due on the field in five minutes to start playing the second half of the game. All of a sudden the door opened and Coach Rockne looked in and said, "Do you know where the Notre Dame football team's locker room is?" Then he turned and walked away. The team charged out the door and the second half was all Notre Dame. They won the game. In this case, a put-down question had been used effectively and the result was very positive.

Another of my all-time favorite examples occurred after the Bay-to-Breakers footrace in San Francisco in May 1985. This is a 12 kilometer run from one side of the city (starting near San Francisco Bay) to the other side of the city (at the Pacific Ocean). The race really is four races. First are the professional world-class runners who are competing for prize money; second are the serious runners who regularly compete on a regional basis; third are people in the race just to have fun who dress up in wild costumes (many just walk), and for them this is just one large moving block party; and fourth are the centipedes. This is a group of thirteen people who are tied together. There are two important requirements; they must be tied together only a few feet apart and they must stay tied for the whole race. Most centipedes do it for fun and wear wild costumes. A few are serious runners, with no costume, who try for record times. The most serious of these groups came from one running club in the Bay Area. These men had been first in the centipede division every year they completed, and in fact they had finished ahead of every single female runner until 1985.

In 1985, Joan Benoit, the gold medal winner in the Los Angles Olympic marathon, entered the race for fun and for the money. Before the race, the men stated that they had beaten all the females in the past and would do it again that year. Joan beat them by a wide margin and was interviewed just past the finish line by a reporter from a local TV station. She turned her head back toward the racecourse and asked a simple question: "Does anyone know where the centipede is?" A great put-down question.

To better understand how to improve our use of these questions, I want to analyze these examples. All contained a very strong message that the speaker wanted to convey. In the first, in Ireland, the message was, "I'm a stronger (better) man than you are and I can hit a golf ball much longer than you can." In the second, at Notre Dame, the message was, "You are not playing football up to your potential." In the last, the message was, "I'm a significantly faster runner than you are."

It is important to remember that after the question was asked, the situation was not over. In the first example, the men continued to play golf together. In the second example, the team played football not only for thirty minutes more that day, but many more games that season. In many question-and-answer situations, once the answer is given everything is finished. If you ask, "What time is it?" and someone answers, "It is 2:27 p.m.," the communication is over. Generally with put-down questions, the situation continues. The person who is put down will react; that is a given. The reaction may be positive or negative, but there will be a reaction. This is important for the reader to consider before asking this type of question.

The response may be delayed for several years. A good example of this occurred a few years ago in a small start-up company in Silicon Valley. A young woman engineer was hired for the electrical engineering department. During her first few days on the job, she sat in on an important negotiation that the purchasing department was conducting with a major supplier. This was a key part of her on-the-job training. No one on the sales side of the negotiation had ever met her, nor had her name been in any of the key correspondence concerning this negotiation. At the start of the negotiation, the seller asked the purchasing manager, "Do you really think that we need a secretary at the negotiating table to take notes? Why don't you ask the secretary to leave?" The purchasing manager responded that she was a new engineer with the company, this was part of her training, and she would be a silent observer. That was the end of that discussion. The response occurred five years later when the engineer took a career-broadening promotion in the purchasing department as the supervisory buyer in charge of purchasing all of the electrical products for the company. How long do you think it took her to stop purchasing from the company that had put her down five years earlier?

Before we review more examples of put-down questions, let's summarize the major points discussed in this section:

1. There is a very strong message that the person asking the question wants to convey.
2. Many times the question is asked of a third party, rather than the person who is the point of the message.
3. After the question is asked, the situation continues and may continue for many years.
4. An emotional response or action (rather than a rational one) is often the result of a put-down question. The emotion may be anger.
5. There may not be a direct oral response to the question.
6. There may not be a direct verbal or oral answer to the put-down question. In most other question situations, there is a direct answer.

Set Up Another Person for the Answer We Want

Examples:

Haven't I been a good mother to you?
How can I be sure that this is the best price anywhere?
Do you know what will happen if you do . . . ?
Do you understand why the CEO made this policy?
Do you know how much you will lose in a divorce?
What will you do for me if I do this for you?

These questions use the same theory. If the other person in a negotiation comes up with the way to get an agreement, that becomes the other person's solution and that person will work hard to make the agreement work. If I try to impose an agreement on the other side, they may resist in the negotiation or they may resist after the negotiation. Since we negotiate to set the ground rules for a future relationship, we want the relationship to be successful. If it is the other person's idea, so what? The main thing is that you achieve the relationship that you need. Having the other person believe that it is his or her idea is a very good tactic.

In reviewing these types of questions, we can see what the objective of the question is and the response we hope to get, and how this will affect the future.

The first question on my list generally would be answered, "Yes, you have been a good mother to me." Next the asker might say, "Then you should understand that I'm doing this for your benefit, not mine." Then the negotiation can become a compromise negotiation.

The other questions are aimed at the same outcome. That is, they get a commitment from the other side that moves the negotiation forward toward a win-win outcome.

Get Others to Sell, Persuade, or Convince Us

Examples:

How do I know that is the lowest price you can give me?
Why should I buy from you and not the competition?
Why do you think you deserve a raise?
What risks are involved in your proposal?

Why should I help you?

Why do you think the stock price will go lower?

Another major use of questions is to get another person to convince us that they are right or that we should take some action. If the question is successful you will, at least, take some action (for example, buy something) and maybe have a strong conviction about a subject that will last for a long time. Remember, the difference between a prejudice and a conviction is that you can explain a conviction without getting emotional or mad.

We generally think of these questions only in buy or sell situations. However, they also can be very important in many other situations or negotiations. All are reviewed in this section. One of the best examples of this type of question, and specifically the answer, was given to me by Hank Calero, who works with many sports and business people. The example was about a football coach. One of the most difficult situations for a football coach is trying to convince a blue-chip high school football player to enroll at the coach's university. This is a hard-sell situation, but it can't appear to be a hard sell. The coach does not want to scare off the recruit, nor the recruit's parents. In many cases, the decision becomes an emotional decision, not a rational decision. This example is a great one to show the positive use of a persuasive question. The situation was related as an example of a win-win attitude, which I very strongly support in all negotiations and other aspects of life.

Here is the background for this example. Each year in the United States there are maybe fifty really outstanding high school football players (hence the term blue chip). These are the people who will make a very significant impact, very possibly for four years, on a college's football program. (Maybe increasing the alumni giving.) Then there are a few hundred players who will be good enough to start the first game of their freshman year and play well. These few hundred may eventually make an all-star team, an all-conference team, or even the All-American team. They will be very good players, but they will not be impact players for that university. The top fifty or so are a big cut above the rest of the very good players. Most of the time they are at the skilled positions. They are not usually linemen, who do most of the hard work but get little credit.

The pressure to recruit blue-chip players is a high priority for the coaching staffs of all college football teams, especially at the big universities where football is king. If a coaching staff can recruit one or two each year, their team will be in the chase for the national championship each year. At the very least, a major bowl bid every year would be guaranteed (with a bonus for the coach). The pressure is also very, very high on the high school player and his family. In many cases, this pressure starts when the player is in his second or third year in high school.

With today's advanced computer systems to keep statistics and all the media attention that sports receive, almost every blue-chip player is known by all coaches. There is tremendous competition for these players. The specific situation I want to share is when UCLA was trying to recruit a six-feet seven-inch, 290-pound lineman. He could play either offense or defense, his time for the 40-yard dash was outstanding, and he was an A–minus student. Some of the many colleges that were trying to sell him on their program were the University of Pittsburgh, Stanford, Baylor, Oklahoma, and Ohio State.

The UCLA coach was the last one to make a presentation to the family. This was a planned tactic. One of the keys to success for the seller is to be the last seller to negotiate with the buyer. I continually stress this when I teach sales negotiation classes and workshops. The last seller only has to beat the best deal currently on the table to win the contract. Most buyers do not want to continue the negotiation any longer than necessary, so if the person they are negotiating with has the best deal, and it is the last negotiation; the buyer will place the order.

The first seller to negotiate with the buyer may not get a second chance to negotiate, so they must put their best offer on the table during the negotiation. They can't leave anything for later because later may never come. There may not be an opportunity for a best and final offer. Their offer may be 1 percent or less too high and they will not get the order. Their offer may be 7 percent too low and they won't make all the profit possible on this order. When there is no opportunity for a second look, these sellers are at a big disadvantage.

The last seller has a different objective in the negotiation. This objective is not to put the best offer on the table but to find out what is the best current offer on the table. So these sellers will do a lot of questioning and probing to get information. They want to "help" the buyer to get the best deal. Once the seller knows the best deal on the table, the seller is able to make a judgment about the offer. This allows the last seller to get the order and make the highest possible profit. The seller does not have to go any lower than necessary.

Key to Success: Be the Last Seller to Negotiate with the Buyer

The UCLA coach was able to use this strategy. It did put pressure on him, because with this advantage he was expected to win the negotiation. He had to come up with an offer (presentation) that was just a little bit better than that of his competition. All of the schools that made their presentations before UCLA were very good schools. They had big-time football programs, went to bowl games almost every year, and had long traditions of excellence. All offered a high-quality education. They were all just outstanding choices. The high school student would be very successful and have a great start in life if he attended any one of these schools. The UCLA coach needed to show how his program was different.

This is another key to success for a seller in negotiations. The seller must be different. An outstanding strategy is called *product differentiation*. For this to occur, these two things must exist:

1. There must be a difference in the product.
2. The difference must be important to the customer.

Here are a couple of examples. First, think of two oranges, one with the word *Sunkist* on it and the other without. Is there a difference? The right answer is yes, there is a difference, because one has Sunkist on it and the other does not. Thus the first requirement for product differentiation is met. Next, if the difference is important to the customer (i.e., the customer believes that Sunkist is better), then a sale is made. The second requirement for product differentiation is also met. Once the seller has established product differentiation, the seller then can command a higher price for the seller's product. Listen to most TV advertisements. Their base is product differentiation. In the case of the oranges, in almost all stores *Sunkist* oranges have a higher price.

Key to Success: Sell Product Differentiation Whenever Possible

When I'm negotiating to present a negotiation workshop for a prospective client, I use product differentiation all the time. I bring copies of the first two books on negotiation that I have published. My hidden sales pitch is, "Do you want to learn from someone who reads the books, or from the person who wrote the books?" Emphasizing that people will be able to learn, in my workshop, from a published author is the way I try to differentiate myself from the other professors and consultants who teach negotiation seminars.

To finish the UCLA example, the coach's problem was made extremely difficult by the ground rules that the player's family had established. After reducing their selection to a final four schools, each school was allowed one last meeting with the family before the decision was made. Each meeting took place in the dining room. When the coach entered that room, the father, mother, the player, and their family lawyer were waiting at the table. The father was at the head of the table, the mother and lawyer on his left, and the player on his right.

Note that I teach in all of my negotiation workshops that the head of any table is the power position. This is true in almost every culture in the world, and people will generally acknowledge this as a fact. This power position can be used to control the negotiation, so I teach that you should sit at the head of the table.

Key to Success: Sit at the Head of the Negotiation Table

The coach took a seat at the other end (the foot) of the table.

Key to Success: If Not at the Head, Sit at the Foot of the Table

After only the briefest small talk, the father took off his watch, put it on the table, and said, "You have twenty-five minutes. Why do you think that our son should attend UCLA?" This was a perfect persuade question. It was open-ended; it did not give the other person any direction for an answer; and it allowed for any type of answer.

"Twenty-five minutes?" the coach said. "It will only take me fifteen. Thank you for the additional time, but UCLA is so far superior that I will not need the extra time." The coach was very careful to take only fifteen minutes. He was very straightforward and to the point. The family's questions took over two hours, and the player enrolled at UCLA.

This is one example that I share with many of my students. It clearly shows how you can ask a very good question to get the information that you need. It is also a great example of how you can turn a challenging question and situation completely to your advantage with the right answer. Another purpose of this book is to show how both sides can win when the question and the answer are the right ones, and to help you learn this very important skill to become a successful negotiator.

This example shows the power of a good question and how it can put pressure on the other person. It also shows that the person answering the question has a lot of power and that person must take advantage of that power. (Remember the starched shirt example earlier in this chapter.)

This example includes many learning points. Let's analyze it from several points. The father wanted to get all of the information possible so that his son could make the right choice for both higher education and football. The family had completed an exhaustive study and had eliminated all but four universities. The family had really been through it all. What new information could they obtain from these last meetings with each team? Not much, but they had to make a choice, so they decided to try a high-pressure question to see what reactions that would get. Their question was a very good example of a pressure convince-me type of question. Later the coach found out that the other schools all went over the allotted twenty-five minutes. This was because their representatives could not give the complete pitch in that short time period.

The UCLA coach recognized that he was in the ideal position (going last), but he also knew that he had to be very good to be better than the others were. He understood that as soon as the question was asked, he had the opportunity to be in the power position. The most important part of his answer would be the first sentence, because it would set the stage for everything that followed. He gave a very aggressive answer. The answer took all of the perceived pressure out of the question and the coach had complete control of the situation. He controlled whether UCLA won or lost the student. This is the ideal position to be in and a position that you must always strive for, because your objective is to control the situation before you win your objectives.

Key to Success: First Control the Situation, Then Go for the Win-Win

In this example, both sides tried to control the interview. The family tried by asking a pressure/convince-me type of question. The coach tried to take control by his aggressive answer, and the coach was successful. I believe that most people would not be as successful as the coach was, and in many situations the family would have controlled the negotiation.

Another important point of this example is that very few people can handle a time deadline, especially in an unstructured situation. Most people plan ahead of time what they will say in a negotiation, or at least the main points of what they will say. This is especially true in hard-sell situations. Time is less important than the message. It is the message that they work on. The outline of the sales pitch, the major points, the opening statement, and especially the close will receive much attention. Very little effort, if any, will be spent on time.

Key to Success: Put Time Limits on the Other Side

Most people are uncomfortable with deadlines, which put added pressure on them. So I encourage the reader to put limits on the time allowed for the answer to your convince-me questions. Put the time first. This will place more attention on the time restriction. Also, I would recommend strong nonverbal communication, such as looking at your watch, to really get the message across to the person on the other side of the table. Remember, the question started, "You have twenty-five minutes."

The question that the father asked had three other very good points. First, the question was addressed directly to the coach when the father said, "Why do you think . . . ?" This should get a personal response, rather than a canned response.

Many sales pitches are memorized. A good example of a canned sales pitch is a story that George Hamilton, a good friend I've worked with on negotiation research and in teaching negotiation workshops, uses the first day in many of his workshops. At that time, George was president of

George Hamilton Associates, a sales consulting firm in Pittsburgh that taught many specialized sales and marketing seminars. The example covers a door-to-door salesperson's first day on the job. During the salesperson's training period, the person had been given a sample script of the typical sales call. The person had memorized this script, knew it by heart, and was ready to make that first sale. At the first house, the salesperson knocked on the door and as soon as the door opened the salesperson said, "Good morning sir or madam, whichever one applies, I'm here to . . ." The problem of course is the words "sir or madam, whichever one applies," which were in parentheses in the script. (I'm sure every reader has had a telephone call from a telemarketer who just read a script and attempted to get a sale without being able to answer any specific questions.) Learn from this and the UCLA example and try to accomplish what the father did, when he said, "Why do you . . . ?"

Second, the question was specific. In many convince-me situations, the question is much too general. Saying "my son" was important. If the question was why should a person attend UCLA, the coach could have given very good reasons that were not to the advantage or interest of the son. For example, the coach could have reviewed the fine medical and music schools at UCLA. Or the coach could have talked about housing in the surrounding neighborhood that would help students who did not have a car. Either of these answers would have had no bearing on the son's situation. Note that the father's question could have been even more specific if he had asked for five (or some other workable number) of reasons. The very best convince-me questions are very specific and ask what you can do for me.

Third, the question could not be answered with a yes or no answer. Consider what might have happened if the question was, "Do you really think that my son should attend UCLA?" The answer could have been "yes," "of course," or something similar. The family would not have had any more information. There probably would have been silence, as the coach would have felt that the question was completely answered and would be waiting for an agreement. The next few minutes could have been a problem for both sides. The whole impact of the question would have been lost, especially the time-limit part, because the question was answered in less than twenty-five minutes. With the next question (and there had to be a next question), would the coach get a new twenty-five-minute time period?

In summary, the question was an example of a good convince-me question because it did four good things: (1) it had a time limit; (2) it asked for a personal answer; (3) it was very specific; and (4) it could not be answered yes or no.

Now to analyze the coach's answer. The coach did several good things with his answer: "Twenty five minutes? It will only take me fifteen. Thank you for the additional time, but UCLA is so far superior that I will not need the extra time." The answer was an "I" answer. The strongest response to a convince-me question is an I answer. I believe that (my product, my idea, my cause, whatever) is right or best. It is hard to argue with a person who has a strong, positive response and is proud of his or her product or cause.

Second, the answer did not put down the father who asked the question. Many times the answer to a convince-me question is to put down the other person, by implying the person is stupid because the person does not understand. The message generally is, "If you weren't so stupid, you would understand and I would not have to explain it to you." This is especially true with people who feel inferior or mistreated by society. The coach not only did not put down the father, but the coach complimented the father.

Third, the answer took the opening given by the question and fit the answer into the prepared presentation. This not only was a good opening but also provided a very good summary, as after the answer the coach listed the major reasons why the son should attend UCLA. The coach closed with, "Based upon these points, I'm sure that you must agree with me that UCLA is far superior, is the best choice for your son, and must be your choice." The coached asked for a commitment.

The coach did four good things: (1) he took control of the situation; (2) he gave an I answer; (3) he did not put down the person who asked the question; and (4) he used his answer as a lead-in to his prepared material.

I really like this example because it is one in which both the question and the answer were very good. Both the question and the answer prove important points about how to ask and how to answer convince-me questions. This does not happen often in life and many times the outcome is not a win-win outcome. This real-life situation ended on a very positive note as the son had a very successful football career and, more important, earned his BS degree at UCLA. Both the school and the person won. I know that a part of this win-win outcome was the successful asking and answering of a convince-me question.

One last point: If you are asked a convince-me question and the question is bad, you may have to rephrase the question to obtain your objectives. I have taught negotiation and management workshops (in many different subjects such as purchasing, accounting, computers, traffic, problem solving, etc.) and seminars in a wide variety of businesses for many years. I work very hard at getting new clients. Often when I meet a potential customer the person asks a question such as, "What is your course?" or "Can we use your course?" or "Is your course a good deal?" I have to change the question to something like, "Can I make the statement that I'm sure that you and your management want to know exactly how this course will help your organization, both in the short run and in the long run?" The reply is yes," which allows me to start on a specific hard sell to get an order.

Convince-me questions are very common in negotiations. They can be very powerful. Remember these keys:

1. Be specific.
2. Don't ask a yes or no question.
3. Ask for an I answer.
4. Use time to your advantage.
5. Put pressure on the other side.
6. Give an "I believe" answer.
7. Don't put the other person down with your question or your answer.
8. Use your answer as the lead-in to a prepared presentation.
9. Always take control of the situation.

This is a powerful area. The savvy negotiator will practice these skills whenever possible and create winning situations in the future.

Attempt to Get Commitments or Promises

Examples:

If I lower my price, will you sign now?
When will you finish reviewing my proposal?
How much will you buy before the price goes up?
Which issue do you think we can agree on first?
Does your spouse have to agree on the color?
Can we agree the price will be between $10.27 and $11.09?

These questions are very similar to the convince-me question, but they expect more. The questions are aimed at closure. They want the other person to provide all the information necessary to convince the asker that it is a good deal, and then move right to closing the deal.

Many of these questions start with *if*. This is a powerful word when used in negotiations, because it is aimed at getting a commitment from the other side without giving a commitment. Let's review an example.

A seller asks, "If I agree to pay the freight on this order, will you give me a purchase order?" The buyer replies, "Yes." Has the buyer made a commitment to the seller? Yes, the buyer has made a firm commitment to the seller because if the seller pays the freight, the buyer will give the seller a purchase order.

Has the seller made a commitment to the buyer? No, the seller said, "If." The seller may say something like, "You know that that is against our corporate policy, but let me talk to my boss and see if the boss will waive the policy for your order." But the seller has gained a major advantage. The seller knows that except for the issue of who pays the freight, the buyer has accepted all of the other terms and conditions of the negotiation.

Key to Success: Use If-Questions to Get Firm Commitments from Others

---

Using if-questions must be a major negotiation tool for all sellers. All buyers must be aware of this tool and must not fall into the trap. In many of our day-to-day negotiations, the seller will use if-questions. There are several variations of the if-question, such as, "What if," "Maybe," or "Can I tell my boss that you will agree to . . . ?"

You must never answer an if-question with a firm statement. When you do, you could be in big trouble because you have given a very firm commitment to the other side without getting anything in return. One of the best ways to respond to an if-question is to use *if* in your response. For example:

SELLER: If we agree to pay the freight, will you give my company a purchase order?

BUYER: If I receive your firm commitment to pay the freight, in writing, I will strongly consider giving you a purchase order.

or

BUYER: When will you know if your company will pay the freight?

or

BUYER: Since you are not certain about your company policy, why don't you call your boss now and get a firm commitment before we continue to negotiate this purchase order?

Key to Success: Never Give a Firm Commitment to an If-Question

---

Identify Specific Needs

Examples:

How badly do you need it?
How close are you to other year-end objectives?
Do airlines that take off late bother you?
Do you love me [looking for a need]?
How often do you run out of inventory?
Does your fiftieth birthday concern you?

A major theme of this book is that savvy negotiators are more needs-oriented negotiators. Our desire must be to satisfy needs on both sides of the table so that we can achieve win-win relationships. This type of question is very important to meet that desire. The satisfaction of someone else's needs is one of the best ways to be successful in life and in the negotiation process. The main problem is determining what the needs are. Remember that earlier we discussed the difference between wants and needs. This section mainly addresses needs. The art of asking and answering the right way is vital. The people involved in the

negotiation can easily become emotional, and that will affect the outcome of the negotiation.

Hank Calero shared this two-liner:

Human hopes and human creeds
Have their root in human needs

The ability to determine another person's needs is most important in
life in general, in all business situations, in all social situations, and, most
important, in all family situations. The key is to determine what are the
needs, not what we think are the needs. One of the major mistakes that
people make is to assume something about another person's needs.

Another mistake that many people make is to project themselves, and
their values, onto other people. We often get into trouble because we
assume we know others' needs and we project what their needs should
be. The savvy negotiator must check each person and each situation before acting, because we all are different and have different needs. This
type of question is very important to your success.

I can't stress enough that you can never assume what the needs are of
the person with whom you are negotiating. This example is one of the
best I know. In the 1960s, a very good friend of mine, Paul, owned a small
business in Ohio that sold gasses (oxygen, hydrogen, etc.) over a five-
county area. He built a very profitable business because he learned to
identify real needs, not perceived needs or assumed needs. He became the
number one supplier of these products, after starting from nothing.
He was able to take a lot of business away from the other suppliers in the
area, many of whom had been in the business for several years. He won
the business; he did not get it by default. How he won a market segment will demonstrate how he used need-development questions to his
advantage.

The market segment was the auto repair business. In the largest town in
his overall market, there were five auto repair companies. They did all
auto repairs, but mostly body and mechanical repair work. Basically these
companies cut, shaped, and welded metal, using a large amount of gas.
Three of the companies were general repair shops that would work on any
type of car that needed repairs. They were close to the same size and each
had one wrecker truck to tow cars to their shop. These repair shops
covered almost all of the five-county area, so their market and the gas

supplier's market were the same. The other two repair shops specialized in foreign car repair work. One was almost 100 percent British (Austin-Healy, MG, Triumph, etc.) and the other shop worked on other foreign cars. All five of the repair shops were small business operations and all were very labor intensive. These shops would purchase new or used parts to repair the cars and would mark up the cost in the final price, but labor was generally the largest component of the final invoice. Labor was also the most important area for cost control, schedule control, and profit improvement. Because all five companies were small, they had to purchase gas in cylinders (their volume was too small to use large tanks at a lower cost). The auto repair companies had been in business from two to twenty-nine years.

The largest gas supplier in the area had been in business for twenty years. During this time, several people had tried to start a competing gas supply company. The terms of sale were standard and were the same for all five auto repair shops. With the lack of competition, these were terms that were acceptable to the gas supplier. The gas supplier offered thirty days net for payment of each invoice, with a 1 percent discount if the invoice was paid in ten days. The gas supplier would deliver six days of the week and make Sunday emergency deliveries if necessary (10 percent additional charge for this service). The gas supplier would deliver to a specific location in each shop, would hook up the new cylinders, and take away the empty cylinders. The price was quoted per 1,000 cubic feet, based upon the volume used per year, and all the shops paid the same price since they all had about the same volume per year. Another charge was for gas cylinder demurrage. This is essentially a rental charge. If a cylinder was at a repair shop for more than thirty days, demurrage was charged at a cost per day. The reason for demurrage was that the gas supplier wanted to have a good turnover of cylinder inventory (fairly standard for the industry).

Paul had started his own gas business in another area of the state. He and his family wanted to move to my area to be closer to Paul's parents. He started a new gas business as soon as he found a suitable building. Then he started a round of first sales calls to introduce his company, find out what needs he could satisfy, and start the task of getting new customers. One call was made at the largest general repair shop. He asked to see the president, and the response was, "Which one?" The owner and president was just retiring and the son was going to be the new president.

The father was in the shop that day, so my friend talked to him first. It was a fairly standard sales call. They talked about the business in general, the specifics of the business in the area, and the problems of the gas business in general. Then my friend talked to the son, but only for a few minutes as the son was very busy. Paul made an appointment for two weeks later to talk to the son.

When the time arrived for the appointment, the father was officially gone and the son was completely in charge. The sales call was made in the only office in the auto repair shop, behind closed doors. My friend sensed that this was unusual. In most circumstances, the discussion would take place in the open shop area, so the boss could watch the workers or show the salesperson problem areas. Using an office was not the norm, so my friend decided to go slowly, and he asked a series of questions about need. He assumed nothing. He started from scratch. He quickly found out that the son knew very little about the auto repair business. A good student and a good athlete, the son had done very well in high school and college and almost all of his time had been devoted to studies and sports. (Knowing the young man, I would expect he also had some fun times.) The father had a serious unexpected health problem and had decided to retire early. The son had spent a little bit of time with the accounting books for the business but knew nothing about how to buy, how to do the actual work, or how to manage in this environment. Since the business really depended upon the performance of the men who did the actual work on the cars, both in quality and time, the secret to being profitable was to manage labor.

The son, even with his MBA, was about to fail because he didn't have any technical metalworking skills and he had not worked in the environment of an auto repair shop. This environment was very different from what the son had been used to all of his life. My friend, through very skillful need questioning techniques, was able to establish these facts. With these facts established, my friend had the keys to success. The new president did not want to fail but knew that his lack of experience and knowledge would lead to a quick death for the company that his father had worked so hard to build into a success. The new president was really desperate but did not want others to know. The real need became apparent only through need-type questions about everything, not just the specifics of the business.

Paul set up a special training program for the son on Sunday afternoons. This included all of the basics of auto repair, welding, and so on, as well as facts about the business in general. This was intense training. The son actually did the welding (although his work was not left in the shop) and some repair work. Within a short time, the son became an accomplished welder, understood the business, and was in a position to manage and control the shop and the business. The proof came a few weeks later when two welders were sick on the same day. The shop had several rush orders that day, so the son, after checking with the other workers to ensure it was acceptable to them for him to do actual work. That he was not threatening their future jobs. He started to do some welding, and his work was first class. That day the son won the respect of his people, and the success of the business was assured. From that time on, Paul got 100 percent of the business, with a long-term contract.

After a few months, Paul found out that his competition had only asked the standard questions during their sales calls with the son. Their main objective was to review the business and any purchase orders that were in force at that time. The father had written these orders. The questions asked were to make sure that the son understood the terms and conditions for the sale of gasses, demurrage, and so on. The competition even followed with a letter to confirm, in writing, the terms and conditions of the past and for the future. These salespersons even reviewed, in depth, their letters, during the next sales call to ensure that there were no problems. This salesperson assumed that the needs of the company with the son in charge were the same as the needs of the company with the father in charge. This was a major mistake.

My friend now had a toehold in the market but needed more customers. The next target was a brand-new company that was formed to do auto repair work by two workers who wanted their own business. They started with almost nothing. They had saved for a few years, but with normal family expenses and only average wages, their nest egg was small. They needed gas to complete their work, but they had a major cash flow problem. Cash flow could break them, and they could lose everything. The competition talked to them, but since they did not have good credit, would not give them extra time to pay their bills. The competition "understood," but "good business practices" would not let the competition change their way of doing business. Paul got 100 percent of the business (whatever it would be), because he determined that the major need was cash flow. Most new businesses have cash flow problems. They do not have any credit, so it is hard for the business to buy parts, materials, and supplies. Auto repair customers sometimes pay in cash and sometimes by credit card, but often the payment is made by an insurance settlement. In those cases, payment takes a long time. The company is out the money it spends for parts and labor, but has no income.

As new owners, these two men were proud, but maybe a little too proud because they did not disclose their need for credit. They wanted to appear to be in control. Paul asked normal questions about the business, but also asked questions about the families and outside activities. He found out that one of the new owners had to take his daughters out of the local soccer program, supposedly because they were tired of soccer. The real reason had to be the cost of soccer. Paul floated the idea of ninety-day terms and received an immediate agreement. The new company was so pleased with these terms that they offered to pick up and return the gas cylinders in their own truck. This saved Paul delivery costs. Again, Paul was able to obtain an order because he asked the right questions.

By asking need questions, Paul was able to become the largest supplier in the area. He found out that a new company that was going to specialize in trucks and off-road vehicles needed to meet local businesspeople, specifically potential customers, and Paul set up these meetings. Other companies heard, by word of mouth, that Paul was a good guy to work with. Why a good guy? The secret was, he knew that taking care of needs is the best way to get business. By asking many questions, he aimed at finding out real needs (not just wants).

This skill of asking the right kind of questions, at the right time to gain information and not put the other side on the defensive, was the key to his success. A very common problem is that people asking a need question ask the question in such a way that the other person becomes defensive and either refuses to give an answer or gives a false answer. In the above case of the new business, Paul's competition asked, I believe, questions that put the new owners on the defensive about their finances. As a result, they lied about how much money they had. Paul did not make them defensive and received the right information to earn many purchase orders.

These examples point out two very important ideas. First, need satisfaction is one of the best ways to be successful in life. Second, asking the right kind of questions is one of the very best ways of determining needs. These questions must not put pressure on the other person. They must encourage and create an open atmosphere.

A story about Marilyn Monroe shows what happens when we do not address real needs but project assumed needs onto others. As she was growing up, Marilyn was moved from one foster home to another many times. Each family gave her food, shelter, clothes, and so on. They took care of what they assumed were her needs. Marilyn learned that wherever she went, she would have food, shelter, and clothes. She did not perceive that she would ever be without these items. What Marilyn really needed was love and recognition, and much of her bad behavior was because she never received love. Her behavior as an adult reflected this need. As she was growing up, related a reporter, she was shuttled between foster families from whom she longed for affection. Once as she was watching a foster mother put on makeup, the woman playfully daubed Marilyn's face with her powder puff. It was a major emotional jolt for me when Marilyn, then a grown woman, told how meaningful that touch had been. Marilyn remembered that incident and whenever she told the story she had tears in her eyes. I often wonder what would have happened if Marilyn's need for love had been satisfied when she was growing up. What would have happened if a foster mother or father had just cared about and asked about her life and found out what Marilyn really needed? She might have lived a long life and made many more very successful movies.

Of course, there are thousands of examples of questions that help identify open needs, but we also want to look for hidden needs. I encourage the reader to look beyond the obvious point or the most obvious area to look for an important need. A friend of mine is into yacht racing and told of a woman that he met in Newport, Rhode Island, during the America's Cup races. This woman was a pretty divorcee from across the bay in a part of Rhode Island known as the Back County. She said the working-class islanders characterized the yachting set as the Red-Pants crowd. Their pants were a special rich color, Breton red, and were distinguished by the inability to keep a crease. The rest of the costume included a blue blazer, white tennis shirt, no socks, and Topsiders for shoes. That was the "official" uniform for the jet set. The woman said that most of the guys hit on her starting out with something like, "Hi. I just got off of my boat. I need a drink, and I want you to have a drink with me." She heard that several times a night. She told my friend, "Everybody who talks to me says that they just got off their boat. If a guy ever said to me, 'I just drove here in my old beat-up Toyota,' I'd be so impressed that I'd buy him drinks all night." The woman's real need was to be treated as an equal, not to get free drinks. The boaters were showing they were superior to her with "I just got off my boat." A person in an old Toyota would be her equal and she would be happy to buy the drinks. Many times a good-looking person does not have to be told about their looks. They know they are good-looking. They have other needs and addressing the other needs is most important.

In summary, this section covers a very important type of question, the need question. The purpose is to have your opponents express their needs (not wants), so that you can understand those needs. Maybe opponents need to confirm the needs to themselves. There are six important points to remember:

1. Need satisfaction is the key to success in all areas of life, especially our day-to-day negotiations.
2. We cannot make assumptions about the needs of other people.
3. Don't always address the most obvious needs.
4. Don't put the other person on the defensive when asking need questions.
5. Always work toward positive results.
6. Always look for win-win agreements.

Key to Success: Negotiate at Your Opponent's Need Level

Key to Success: Separate Needs from Wants

Display Our Intelligence

Examples:

When I taught at the university, we learned X. Do you agree?
Did you study negotiation like I did in my MBA program?
I belong to the honor society. Do you?
Have you studied X in depth like I have?
Do your ideas come from the masters, as mine do?
With my background, why do you disagree with me?

It is very true that people will ask a question to show how smart they are. Generally this does not accomplish anything positive and many times the result is negative. It could easily turn off the other person. Also it is possible that the other person can top the first person. For example, the answer to the second question might be, "Yes I did study negotiation in both my MBA and PhD programs."

It is suggested that the savvy negotiator will avoid these types of questions whenever possible, because they accomplish little and may create a bad feeling in your opponent. When they are used against you, try to stay calm and keep control of the situation.

Test Assumptions

Examples:

Is the price of gas the reason you are buying a small car?
You believe that blue is your best color, right?
Do you believe low price is nothing, if it is late?
I doubt that you will drive a lot on the snow.
I assume you deal with the EPA in San Jose.
Are casual suits best for dress-down Friday?

Many people have attended training courses where they learned never to use the word *assume*. They were told that if you assume, you make an *ass* (of) *u* (and) *me*. This is not true in negotiations, because in the negotiation planning process, we must make many assumptions. For example, we make assumptions about the other side's need and wants, the strategies they will use, how hard they will press their points, and so forth.

In the planning of any negotiation, assumptions must be made. The savvy negotiator must test the assumptions, made in the planning phase of the negotiation, during the actual negotiation and these questions are very, very important for successful negotiations. Most successful people will identify the assumptions in their plans and will write out specific questions to test these assumptions.

For example, a buyer in an industrial negotiation may want to ask the supplier to stock finished materials or products for the buyer. The buyer is not sure what it will cost the supplier (interest rate), so the buyer needs to find out what the current cost of money is to the supplier. During the planning phase of the negotiation, the buyer assumes the interest rate is 7.2 percent. During the early part of the actual negotiation, the buyer may ask, "Were you able to obtain a long-term line of credit before the rates went up?" When the seller answers, the buyer now has a good idea of the interest cost of stocking materials and is able to use this later in the negotiation when the buyer asks for a stocking program.

> **Key to Success:** Questions Are a Good Way to Test Assumptions

Probe Further, Explore, and Get Additional Information

Examples:

Is price the only area still open for negotiation?
If blue is your best color, which is your best style?
Besides your salary, what other needs do you have?
How many real issues haven't we discussed yet?
Are these fares good for both winter and summer?
How much more will you reduce the price?

Many times when information is given, as a result of a question, the person only gives part of the complete answer. Many times the answer is a half-truth. In negotiations we define half-truth as a statement that is completely true, but does not tell the whole truth. For example, a person could ask, "Did the San Jose Earthquakes win a soccer game last night?" The answer is "No." What happened to the Earthquakes? One, they could have lost. Two, they could have tied. Three, they might not even have played a game. The answer "No" is correct for all outcomes, but does not tell the whole story. Savvy negotiators listen and understand that when they hear a half-truth, they must ask more questions. In these cases, the answer does not satisfy the question asked, nor does it end the discussion about that point. The answer is not complete, or the answer is limited. A follow-up question is required. The purpose of these questions is to get more information without causing conflict. How the question is asked is very important. Also, all of the nonverbal communications must be open and outgoing. The question should not seem to be a put-down.

Draw Attention to Yourself

Examples:

Do you understand how badly I need . . . ?
What's in the deal for me, personally?
My first reaction has not changed. Why has yours?
Don't you think that was my best shot of the day?
Do you know anyone who has my good looks?
How do you like living next to me, . . . ?

In many situations in life, a person feels left out of the process or the decision. The normal reaction is to get very angry, to get attention and to get back in the process. The person may verbally attack the other person or some nearby physical thing. Normally, all this behavior accomplishes is to start a conflict or to raise the conflict level of that situation. It often becomes a lose-lose situation.

People need another way to behave. These questions provide the possibility of getting attention without creating a conflict situation. These should always be the first option, when you feel left out.

Also, such questions can establish your position (for example, as an expert) without blowing your own horn.

Key to Success: Questions Can Help to Avoid Conflict

Evade Questions

Examples:

Can't we discuss that issue later in the negotiation?
I'm not sure how to answer that question.
How can we discuss price before all the other issues?
Would your boss think that is an appropriate question?
How can you ask about B before we have agreed on A?
Is 0 to 60 really important driving in New York City?

Thousands of times in life, people are asked questions they do not want to answer. Generally, the answer will put the person at a disadvantage.

The above are a few of the thousands of questions you can ask to avoid answering a problem question. This is a way to put the ball back in the other court.

Children are very good using this type of question and adult negotiators must also learn to be very good to maximize their position in their negotiations.

Control the Other's Behavior

Examples:

When will you act like an adult?
Why does a missed putt upset you so much?
Do you want to take a break and get control of yourself?
(To person A) How long does B usually act like that?
Is throwing things professional behavior?
If you don't stop, do you know what will happen?

Many people will react negatively when they are given direct orders or suggestions to change their behavior. They may believe their behavior is OK, or they may believe the other person does not have the right to tell them what to do. This type of question aims at overcoming this resistance by allowing the other person to make the decision to change. These questions have the potential to be very powerful.

Allow Others to Use Their Insight

Examples:

Why don't you review all of our agreements?
Do you see any hidden problems?
Is there a creative way to solve this impasse?
Does your experience shed any light on this problem?

Each of us likes to believe we have important things to say. How often have you heard the expression "not invented here"? We are able to avoid this problem by asking questions to get the other person to "invent the idea" and then to make it work.

Get Reassurance for Ourselves

Examples:

Do you love me?
Will you always stay with me?
Haven't I added profit to this company?
Will I be able to work till my normal retirement age?
Is this a good golf swing?

People often are reluctant to show fear or weakness. They need to have these fears reduced to be able to be productive. Once these fears are reduced, the person should be ready to negotiate and look for a win-win agreement. It is very difficult to look for a win-win if there is a lot of fear of the other side. A question, many times, is a safer way to achieve this purpose. A savvy negotiator will recognize the need, address it, and provide necessary reassurance. Once fear is reduced, the negotiation can move forward toward an agreement.

Discover Specific Feelings, Emotions, or Beliefs

Examples:

How do you feel inside right now?
Why are you so mad?
Do you believe in an afterlife?
Are you pro-life?
What is your deepest fear?
Do you think President Ford was a good president?

Questions about emotions or beliefs are very hard for some people to ask. Many times that is because people do not want to answer a similar question about themselves. Also, many people do not know how to deal with strong personal feelings. Feelings and emotions are a very significant part of most interpersonal negotiations and must be addressed. You must be able to ask these types of questions to be able to have successful win-win personal negotiations.

Find Areas of Mutual Agreement or Compromise

Examples:

Can we agree on section one (out of nine) of the proposal?
In which area do you believe our positions are the closest?
Do you like anything about my proposal?
We should start on the easiest issue. Which one is it?

Negotiations are settled on an incremental basis. A person does not move from his or her initial position in one giant leap to an agreement. Negotiators move toward each other in small steps. These questions are aimed at helping to take these small steps. With several small agreements (or agreements on small issues), the negotiators have a much better foundation on which to negotiate and come to agreement on the larger issues.

Isolate Areas of Disagreement

Examples:

If we can settle on the price, do we have a deal?
Besides the terms, do you have any other problems with my quotation?

Since negotiations are settled on an incremental basis, a key to success is to isolate those areas of disagreement. This is very powerful if only a few issues are left to be discussed. People should focus on how close they are to agreement. For example, "Jack, we have complete agreement on twenty-five of the twenty-seven issues in this negotiation. Should we let small differences on the final two issues ruin the deal?"

Get the Opponent's Attention

Examples:

Do I have to go to your boss to get an answer?
Where is your mind right now, on a golf course?

People negotiate best when they are completely involved in the negotiation. Many times people tend to drift in and out of the negotiation.

Their attention span may not be very long. You may have to get your opponent back to the table with this type of question. Another problem is that sometimes people don't understand what will happen if the negotiation fails. A question, rather than a harsh statement, may be best to bring them back. The reminder should come out as a question, not as a sharp attack or a chewing out.

Divide the Opponent's Team

Examples:

Pam, do you really believe what your leader just said?
Jim (husband), can you afford what Janie (wife) just asked for?
Jean (parent), do you believe a 400-horsepower car is appropriate for Mike (child) to drive?

A major tactic in any negotiation is to divide and then conquer the other side. I'm told by car salespeople that they love to see a husband and wife come in together to buy a car. Since the husband and wife do not have the same objectives, the salesperson is able to divide the "team" and get a higher price for the car or sell a higher-priced car. These car salespeople really get excited when a parent and child buy a car together, because rarely are the two looking for the same things in a car. Rather than try to divide by statements, it is best to divide the other side by using questions.

Eliminate Semantic Traps or Problems

Examples:

What does a smooth surface mean to you?
What is the meaning of *is*?

The meaning of words causes many problems every day of our lives. In negotiations, we are trying to satisfy our needs and we are setting the ground rules for a future relationship. In the future, for your needs to be met, the other side must take some action. We want to be assured that the other side understands what actions are needed. This means the other side's understanding of the words we use must be consistent with our needs. I was involved in a major negotiation in which the first few pages of the contract were a dictionary. This section started, "For the purpose of this contract the following words will be defined as."

The best example I can share is three simple words: "a clean room." The definition of a clean room to a parent and to a child are generally very different.

Restate or Clarify a Position (Yours or Your Opponent's)

Examples:

As I understand your answer, all of your products will receive the same discount. Am I correct?

Since you didn't give fares for winter and summer, they must be the same.

I'm sure that you will always support your favorite team.

Since you agreed to a price reduction and didn't specify the percentage, I'm sure that it will be 10 percent just like the last time you reduced prices.

For my education, would you please expand on the reasons for your current demand?

I need more information to help me understand why your principal wants you to take that position.

This is another type of question whose purpose is to get more information without causing conflict. You will be best served if you do not try to put pressure on your opponent or imply that your opponent is hiding anything. It is always best to make the lack of understanding your fault, not your opponent's fault. Like many other questions, this type of question aims at getting more information. However, instead of asking for it in a very direct manner, the question tries to soften the impact. Also, the asker takes more of the responsibility for the "poor communication." This is a key point.

Key to Success: Use "I Don't Understand" to Get More Information

---

Set a Deadline for Action or Agreement

Examples:

Do you understand we will raise prices on the first?

When do you have to place this order?

Some people will just take a long time to reach an agreement. Others use time as a tactic. To get the negotiation moving along, the savvy negotiator should consider this type of question.

Get Opponent to Agree to a Premise

Examples:

Can we agree that ... ?
I assume your need is ... ?

We can get into major problems in negotiations if the sides are not on the same page or if their assumptions about the situation are different. We often have to make assumptions in the planning of a negotiation. These must be tested during the negotiation.

Make a Point When You Know the Answer

Examples:

Do you know what time it is?
Do you know what will happen if you break your grandmother's favorite cut-glass dish?
Do you understand why we have a conflict of interest policy for this purchasing department?
Do you know how much you will lose if your husband files for separate maintenance?

In many situations in life, we want to make a very strong point to another person. There are times when a person wishes to admonish someone and they can do so very easily by asking a question, instead of making a statement. Rather than making a statement, many times it is better to ask a question (even when you know the answer and in most cases the other person also knows the answer). Questions of this type will almost always generate a response and the asker will get confirmation that the opponent at least heard the point.

For example, someone has just arrived at the office at 10 a.m., instead of being on time at 8:30 a.m. The boss sees this person and asks out loud, "Do you know what time it is?" This is a very strong message saying *you are late*. Sometimes the admonishment might also bring along a qualifier such as, "Must you always be late for work?" or "Can't you be here on time for a change?" Such derogatory questions, which really are statements of fact, make a strong point. Most people are either so embarrassed or upset that they seldom have a good comeback, and alibis are rarely effective.

When you ask these questions, you must be very sure that the question is phrased correctly. Also, the question must be asked from a rational viewpoint, not an emotional viewpoint. A bad question could really hurt the asker.

This real-world example happened to the me many times when I lived in Pittsburgh. One of the approaches to downtown from the south goes through the Fort Pitt tunnel. (When drivers complete the trip through the tunnel, they see a fantastic view of the city. It is a very special sight, leaving the dark tunnel and going into the light and seeing a major city right in front of you.) Several routes converge on the tunnel. About a half-mile before the tunnel, the two right lanes become exit lanes for a route that goes east. The two left lanes go into the tunnel. There are large signs over each lane that give directions. The signs over the right lanes, in large letters, say, "EXIT ONLY." Many aggressive drivers drive in the exit lanes for several yards before merging into a left lane. Our neighbor across the street always went by the letter of the law. When I would drive him into Pittsburgh (as an aggressive driver), I'd be in the exit lane for some time. Every time he would get upset and say in a loud voice, "Don't you know this is an exit lane?"

Pave the Way for a More Important Question

Examples:

Now that these issues are settled, can we talk about price?
Do you want to discuss anything else before we negotiate the last three points?

A good negotiation strategy is to take care of the small issues first. Usually the smaller issues are easier to solve than the big issues. Having agreement on some issues helps to lead to agreement on other issues. These questions are ensuring that all of the small issues are out of the way and the negotiators are ready to discuss the big issues.

Sidestep a Question, but Not to Anger Your Opponent

Examples:

Don't you agree that it is best to address that issue later in the negotiation?
Do you want the complete information on that issue? If so, shouldn't we wait
   until I can get all the facts?

These questions attempt to get the other side to make the decision to
avoid an issue for a while. If you say, "I don't want to discuss that now," it
may cause more conflict. If you can get the other side to make that
decision, there isn't any conflict.

Bring a Discussion to a Close

Examples:

If I agree to give you X, do we have a deal?
What color do you want your car to be?
When should we deliver X to you?

These questions are the classic "closers" that salespersons are taught
on their first day in sales school. We all have heard them and used them.

In team negotiations there is a special way to handle questions, which
is covered at the end of this section.

When considering these questions, you can improve your negotiation
results by remembering four points. First, these questions can be very
powerful, especially when they give information. Because they can be very
powerful, they must be asked only after some careful consideration. It is
very possible that the response, verbal or nonverbal, will escalate the
negotiation or conflict situation. Many times the risk is not worth the
possible reward.

Second, in most life situations, you will deal with someone that you will
deal with many times in the future, a relationship that is probably important
to you. If that is the case (remember that we negotiate to set the ground rules
for a future relationship), I believe that you should ask, "Is this put-down
question worth it in the long run?" before you ask a put-down question.

Third, another consideration is that you may not get the response you
expect or want. The situation may get out of hand or go in a very

unplanned direction. In the football example, the players might have responded, "If the coach has given up on us, why should we try?" and lost the game. If you ask the question, "Do you think I'm an idiot?" the answer may be, "Yes." Or it might be even stronger: "No, I don't think you are an idiot, I know that you are an idiot." Now the ball is in the asker's court, and the ball is coming very fast. The question, "Haven't I been a good parent to you?" could be followed by "No" with a long list of examples that prove the point. In this case, the objective of making the child feel guilty turns around in a few seconds to a situation where the parent feels guilty and loses control of the situation. In negotiation situations, this can be a very powerful tool. These types of questions can give a lot of information is a short period of time. However, they must be used as a positive and rational tool, not a negative and emotional tool.

Fourth, when you answer a put-down question, you have an opportunity to change the direction of the negotiation. In the book *The Human Side of Negotiations*, I listed a large number of personal behaviors needed to be a successful negotiator. One of these is to be a thinking (rational) person, not a feeling (emotional) person. There is a very big difference between a thinking-feeling person (who thinks first) and a feeling-thinking person (who feels first). In negotiations, feeling-thinking people are at a big disadvantage, because they react on an emotional basis. They do not objectively or rationally think about what the correct reaction should be. They just react. Thinking-feeling people think about the correct reaction. They think about the situation and they make a rational decision about the right behavior to obtain their objectives.

When answering put-down questions, it is critical that you answer after thinking about what the correct response would be. If you just blurt out an answer because you have lost control of your emotions, you have lost control of the situation, and a very negative result could happen. Think before you respond to put-down questions. In many cases, the question is asked to get a fast emotional response. Don't let the other person get you.

In summary, put-down questions, can be a very powerful tool in negotiations. However, you must give careful consideration before you ask a put-down question and before you answer a put-down question. Once the question is asked and the answer is given, there may not be a way to turn back.

ALTERNATIVES AVAILABLE WHEN QUESTIONS ARE ASKED

Many alternatives are available when a question is asked. My study of the negotiation process shows that most people only use a very few. Listed below are just a few ways that someone can respond to a question:

Answer the question.
Don't answer the question.
Ask a question in return.
Reword the question.
Challenge the question.
Ask for the reason behind the question.
Defer it for later.
Ignore the question.
Don't answer, but tell the other person why.
State that you can't answer the question.
Ask the other person to repeat the question.
Ask the other person to restate the question.
Ask the other person what answer he or she wants to hear.
First praise the question, then answer it.
First praise the question, then don't answer it.
Respond to an earlier question.
Respond to an unasked question.
Tell them you have already answered the question.
Tell them they know the answer, so why should you respond?
Laugh at the question.
Give a ridiculous answer.
Be silent.
Relay the question to another person on your side.
Relay the question to another person on the other side.
Give a nonverbal response (positive or negative).

ANSWERS THAT CAN CAUSE MAJOR PROBLEMS

There are two types of answers that really cause problems in any negotiation: (1) the complete lie, and (2) the half-truth. The complete lie is a real problem, but generally with specific follow-up questions it can be uncovered. Complete lie answers are usually apparent. They just seem too good to be true, or they provide information that goes against information that the negotiator already knows. The next section covers a very important skill to be a successful negotiator: being very skeptical. The material will provide examples of how we must ask as many questions as necessary to get to the absolute truth. The complete lie generally is easier to detect than the half-truth.

The half-truth is a much bigger problem. A half-truth is a statement that is absolutely true, but the statement does not tell the whole truth. Too many times we hear what we want to hear and accept the answer as the whole truth, and later in the negotiation or relationship we get into trouble. Some examples of half-truths:

Question: "Did the U.S. soccer team win last night?
Answer: "No."
This answer is true for any one of three outcomes. The USA team lost, tied, or didn't play.

Question by student: "Did my paper fulfill all the requirements?"
Answer by professor: "Yes."
This answer is true even if the content in the paper is wrong.

Question by wife: "Do you like this dress?"
Answer by husband: "Yes."
This is true even if the husband likes the dress but he thinks it looks terrible on his wife.

Statement by salesperson: "You should buy the extended warranty; more customers than ever are buying it."
This is true if now 2 percent of the customers are buying, when last year 1 percent purchased it. The real truth is 98 percent do not buy it.

Statement: "This is the lowest price we have ever quoted."
What is not said is "for this specific item, at this specific time, for this specific customer."

Sign in a gas station in Indiana, in the late 1990s: "Buy now last station in Indiana last gas at $1.27 per gallon."
What is not said is that in Ohio the gas is $1.14 per gallon.

Again, half-truths are statements that are true, but do not give the whole truth. Political campaigns are full of half-truths and so are negotiations. In both cases, the people that accept the half-truth statement as a fact get themselves into big trouble.

HOW TO IMPROVE ASKING AND ANSWERING TECHNIQUES

A key to improving your skill at asking and answering questions is to first improve your listening skills. This point was made earlier in this chapter: When we are listening, we are receiving information. When we are talking, we are not receiving information. In this section, I review these ideas:

- The laser approach
- Writing out questions before the negotiation
- Always think before responding

The laser approach requires the negotiator to continue to ask questions until the complete truth is on the table. A key is to hear what is not said. Then ask another question to get more information. In the third example above, the wife should have heard what was not said, "I like the dress on you," and asked a second question. In the fourth example above, the customer should have asked, "Exactly what percentage of your other customers have purchased the warranty?"

Key to Success: Hear What Is Not Said

Writing out questions before the negotiation ensures that you ask exactly what you want to ask, to get the exact information you need. Many answers are half-truths. It is also the case that many questions provide the opportunity to get away with a half-truth answer. After you write out the question, say the question aloud to hear how it will sound to your opponent in the negotiation. Even better, ask a friend or peer to evaluate the question before the negotiation starts. This quick review could provide many positive returns during the negotiation.

Key to Success: Write Out Questions Before Negotiating

One of the biggest problems for every negotiator is the quick response. We talk before we think. This usually gets us into trouble. Mary, a friend of mine, has the letters LT on the face of her watch, so that every time she checks her watch, she is reminded to listen and think before talking.

The very best example of thinking before responding comes from baseball. A few years ago, the major league baseball umpires were unhappy with their labor contract. A clause in this contract would not allow them to strike during the season. Their union leader decided on a unique strategy to put pressure on management to give the umpires a better contract. All of the umpires would send a letter of resignation to baseball headquarters effective early in September. Then baseball would not have the best umpires available during the last month of the regular season (when all of the playoff teams are decided) or during the actual playoffs and World Series. A reporter heard about this strategy and called Sandy Alderson at baseball headquarters. At that time, Sandy was the executive responsible for the umpires. Sandy indicated that before responding he would like to take a few minutes to check out the facts and he would call the reporter back. During the time that he was checking the facts, he was also thinking about his response. The fifteen-word response was so powerful that the union strategy failed and the union was destroyed.

The response was, "That is either a threat to be ignored, or an offer to be accepted."

What a powerful statement! Whatever leverage the union had before that statement was completely lost. By taking time to think about his response, Alderson was able to make the perfect response.

Key to Success: Always Avoid a Quick Response

THE FIVE TOUGHEST QUESTIONS

As part of the research for this chapter, many people were asked to share the five toughest questions that they have ever been asked. A few of the answers are listed below and I'm sure that you will be able to relate to many of these. My question was asked in negotiation workshops, in college classrooms, on international airline flights, of family members, of peers, and of total strangers. Each person was told that it was research for a book and that their name would never be used in the book. In seminars, they put their papers on a separate desk so that I didn't know which questions came from which people. Most people were very cooperative and wanted to help. They felt good that their opinion was important.

It is interesting that perception is so important. Many of these questions I would find very easy to answer and I wonder why anyone would put the question on the list. Many times one of the answers to my question was, "What are the five hardest questions you have ever been asked?" I'm sure that for many people this was an honest answer; for others it was a way to give only four responses. Here are some of the responses to my research. Several questions were given by many people, such as these:

Will you marry me? (most common response)
Will you take this man to be your lawfully wedded husband?
Do you really love me?
What makes you think that you deserve a raise?
Why do you smoke?
Tell me about yourself.
What qualifies you for this job?
Do you have full responsibility for this project?
Do you have full authority to negotiate for your company?
How can you think about striking this airline and hurting your very good customers?
Is it true what they say about pilots and flight attendants on overnight stays?
What does your spouse say about all your traveling?

When I reviewed all of the answers to "What are the five toughest questions you've ever been asked?" the answers fell into one of these areas:

Looking for personal information
Either/or
Third party
My opinion
No win
Irrelevant
What if
Emotional
Using emotional words

Incorrect logic
You must agree

My research shows that the number one toughest question is a question that we do not have an answer to or that we do not want to answer. The reader must be aware of these questions before asking them. The result of asking one of them may be a failed negotiation.

OTHER OBSERVATIONS

There are several additional ideas that I've collected in the area of asking and answering questions that I'd like to share with you. First, the wording of a question can sometimes change the answer. Here's an example from management classes I've taught:

1. You've decided to see a Broadway play and have bought a $75 ticket. As you enter the theater, you realize you've lost your ticket. You can't remember the seat number, so you cannot prove to management that you bought a ticket. Would you spend $75 for a new ticket?

2. You've reserved a seat for a Broadway play for which the ticket price is $75. As you enter the theater to buy your ticket, you discover you've lost the $75 you had in your pocket to buy the ticket. Would you still buy the ticket (assuming you had enough cash or a valid credit card)?

Answer both questions before reading further.

What is your answer to the first question?
What is your answer to the second question?

In their analysis, researchers found that despite the fact that both cases involved the loss of $75, most people would buy a ticket after losing the cash, but not after losing the ticket.

Public opinion pollsters already know that the wording of a question is tremendously important when taking a sample of popular opinion. Depending on how a particular question is worded, the results will be very different and maybe incorrect. Most people do not have the time to spend properly wording each and every question, but they always seem to have time to explain and apologize when their questions upset or offend others.

SUMMARY

When I was very young and attending grammar school, the teachers made statements such as, "You must ask questions to learn," or "Questions are the root of most intelligence," and so on. You can surely remember your personal experiences during this difficult time in life and recall similar statements. The very unfortunate circumstances, however, were that teachers did not give any good instructions on how to ask questions, nor on how to answer them. Apparently they must have thought that the ability to ask and answer questions was born into everybody and that they didn't have to help their students develop the skill and expertise to learn this key part of life. How sad!

When we were very young, in the "why" phase of life, questions served to bring us an understanding of this world and its wonders. Notice how often children ask this question all by itself. Also notice that most of children's longer questions start with *why*. For example, "Why does a match go out, Dad, when you blow on it?"

Approximately fifty years after my grammar school days, I've realized that most of us still know very little about this subtle and skillful art. If you went to your favorite bookstore, in person or on the Internet, and looked at books available that covered the subject of communication, you would be amazed at the large number of them. However, try to find a book, article, college course, seminar, lecture, or any other source on the subject of asking and answering questions and you will again be surprised, not by the amount but by the lack of them. I believe that it is very strange that somehow this part of the communication process has either been over-looked or considered unimportant. This chapter has tried to teach these skills that we should have learned a long time ago and make us more proficient in the art and science of asking and answering questions.

This chapter has covered many topics: seven areas and twenty-seven different types of questions. Again this is the basic outline of the chapter:

1. Examples of bad questions and their results
2. Purpose and types of questions
3. Alternatives available when questions are asked
4. Answers that can cause major problems
5. How to improve asking and answering techniques
6. The "five toughest questions"

7. Other observations
8. Summary

You may think that some of these categories could or should be combined and I do not have a major problem with that position. I do feel that by being as specific as possible, I have opened your mind to the many ways that questions can be used in all our negotiations, especially our day-to-day negotiations.

CHAPTER 4

Ethics and Negotiations

In chapter 2, "Winning Concepts," the first key idea reviewed was that we negotiate to set the ground rules for a future relationship. The second was that we negotiate to satisfy our needs. We also discussed that in most win-lose negotiations, the loser will try to get even during the relationship. Losers will have a very large incentive to get even if they feel their opponent's behavior was unethical during the negotiations. I believe that a person can be a tough negotiator without being an unethical negotiator. Almost all negotiators will respect an opponent who is tough but ethical, and they will disrespect any negotiator who is unethical. For the savvy negotiator, this respect will carry over during the relationship and should make it a win-win relationship.

A good example of this attitude occurred in 1988 during the presidential primary season. Early that year, many people felt that Lee Iacocca should run for the Democratic presidential nomination. This was several years after Iacocca "saved" Chrysler from chapter 11 bankruptcy by obtaining government loans and by obtaining very hard-fought wage concessions from the auto workers' union. There was a short article in *USA Today* in which Iacocca listed his dream cabinet including "former United Auto Workers President Douglas Fraser for Labor 'or, even better, Fraser as chief trade negotiator. (He does know how to negotiate–take my word for it.)'" Fraser had been a tough negotiator representing his union when Fraser negotiated with Iacocca and now Iacocca wanted Fraser to represent him at the negotiating table. This is the ultimate mark of respect.

In the early twenty-first century, there are far too many examples of unethical behavior from both the business world and the academic world.

A few examples are listed below. Note that some type of negotiation (direct or indirect) was involved in each situation, and the unethical behavior had a lasting effect on the parties involved in the negotiation, and sometimes on innocent people not directly involved.

CURRENT BUSINESS EXAMPLES

To demonstrate the problems in the industrial world in the late twentieth and early twenty-first centuries, we need to review only three examples. It is my personal belief that these three situations involve very unethical behavior.

In January 2000, *Fortune* magazine named Enron the most innovative company in the United States and ranked it among the best 100 companies to work for in the U.S. Later, when news was leaked of possible problems in the company, Enron's credit rating was downgraded and both creditors and investors panicked. Less than two years later, Enron declared the largest corporate bankruptcy in the history of the world. By late 2002, Enron was being investigated by five different federal organizations: the Commodity Futures Trading Commission, the Federal Energy Regulatory Commission, the U.S. Department of Labor, the Securities and Exchange Commission, and the Justice Department. It also was being investigated by several states, among them California, which claimed that Enron had overcharged it by several billion dollars during its energy crisis.

It is absolutely clear that Enron's death resulted from a complete lack of ethical practices by the company's top management. The company suffered from mismanagement and an unhealthy business climate that encouraged looking for and finding loopholes in the law to justify the actions of top management. Enron used subsidiaries it controlled and off-the-balance-sheet financing to inflate the company's profit and to report reduced debt.

Another factor in Enron's failure was the fact that Enron's employees reported (as all of the facts were being revealed to the press) that they knew of individual transactions that were intended to make the financial picture look better. These people were isolated and had no idea that similar transactions were widespread throughout the company. Finally, when some employees tried to warn their bosses and top management of problems, they were not taken seriously and some were removed from their jobs.

Millions of people in the United States were significantly hurt by Enron's actions. First were loyal employees who had invested most of their retirement savings in Enron stock. Employees in their fifties and sixties will never have a chance to recover their losses. Additionally, most lost their jobs at a time when the business climate in the United States did not offer a large number of opportunities to start new careers. Second were the stockholders who believed the statements made by top management and lost almost all of their investment in the company. Third were customers who paid more than they had to for Enron services. Fourth and last was the general public, who lost confidence in American business.

A second company that failed was Arthur Andersen. It was Enron's auditor and went out of business as a result of the Enron debacle. Andersen was investigated for its failure to warn the investing public of Enron's problems, and it was found guilty of obstruction of justice. Andersen had attested that Enron's accounts and all of Enron's reports were an accurate representation of Enron's financial position.

Earlier, when individual auditors at Andersen raised questions about the financial and business practices at Enron, they were removed from the Enron account, significantly impacting their careers. Andersen was making millions as a consultant to Enron and didn't want to lose this income. It is estimated that 90 percent of the revenue Andersen made from Enron was from consulting and only 10 percent from auditing.

Another example of unethical behavior involves the investment industry. It is a well-known fact that analysts have often duped investors, advising them to buy stocks that the analysts privately felt should be avoided and sold. This behavior helped the analysts' investment banker friends (or in some cases the investment banking divisions of the companies they worked for) win lucrative (millions of dollars) stock-underwriting assignments and increase the annual bonuses for the analyst, the banker, and the partners of the firm. Since this practice has been highlighted in the press, I believe it is happening a lot less these days.

One example of this unethical behavior involved Citigroup, AT&T, and the Ninety-second Street Y in New York City. It began when the Citigroup CEO asked an analyst to take a fresh look at the analyst's neutral rating for AT&T (at that time, the CEO sat on the AT&T board and the AT&T president sat on the Citigroup board). The analyst indicated that he might change his rating and later asked the CEO to help him get his kids (twins) into an elite nursery school (the Ninety-second Street Y) in New York. The school takes sixty-five children per year, a very small percentage of all of the applicants. A few weeks later, the analyst upgraded his rating of AT&T to a buy. A couple of months later, AT&T decided to give a large contract to Citigroup to underwrite a new tracking stock offering. This contract had a value of almost $45 million. Then, a few months later, Citigroup gave a million-dollar donation to the Ninety-second Street Y where the analyst's children were enrolled. In this example:

1. AT&T won a buy rating for its stock from a very influential analyst, increasing the stock price at an important time for AT&T.
2. Citigroup won a large underwriting fee.
3. The Ninety-second Street Y won a million-dollar donation.
4. The analyst won, getting his kids into the elite nursery school.

This sounds like a win-win-win-win situation. But it was not, because there was a very large number of losers. These losers were the investors who believed the analyst and purchased AT&T stock at inflated prices. The rest of the story is that less than two months after the analyst's twins entered the nursery school, the analyst downgraded his rating of AT&T stock.

CURRENT ACADEMIC EXAMPLES

Unfortunately, there are far too many examples of unethical behavior in the academic world. It is my personal belief that the seven that follow from the academic world will make the point that important improvements must be made in today's educational system. The leaders of tomorrow are being educated in the academic world today. This education must include more than just a few mentions of ethics in general business classes that hardly make an impact on the students. This education must also involve many ethical role models of people who work in all levels of education.

On page 3E of the October 26, 2002, edition of the *San Jose Mercury News*, there was a short article titled "Religious Schools Don't Ensure Ethics." The article reviewed a survey of the ethics of students in public and private high schools in the United States. Significant results of the Josephson Institute for Ethics study were as follows:

- Overall, 74 percent of high school students reported they had cheated at least once on an exam in the past year.
- In 2000, the percentage was 71 percent.
- In 1991, the percentage was 61 percent.
- During the twelve-year period from 1991 to 2002, the number of students cheating on exams increased by more than 20 percent.
- Also, 78 percent of students in private religious schools said they had cheated on an exam in the last year.
- Finally, 72 percent of students in other schools said they had cheated.

The article included this quote from Michael Joesphson, institute president:

> The evidence is that a willingness to cheat has become the norm and that parents, teachers, coaches and even religious educators have not been able to stem the tide. The scary thing is that so many kids are entering the workforce to become corporate executives, politicians, airplane mechanics and nuclear inspectors with the dispositions and skills of cheaters and thieves.

The University of Virginia has a very strong honor code. It was broken by more than 100 students in one science class just a few years ago. One result of this cheating was the subsequent development of new software for professors to check work turned in by their students. This software is currently used by many professors at San Jose State University, where I teach, and many other colleges and universities.

At Stanford University (one of the most elite universities in the world) in Palo Alto, California, in the late 1990s, there was a large cheating scandal during midterm exam week. Midterm exams that year were scheduled the week before spring break, and a few students had their next to last exam on Tuesday and their last exam on Friday. If they took the last exam early they would have a much longer spring break, so they asked the professor if he would let them take the exam early. He did. When the professor graded the exams taken on Friday, all of the other students scored 100 percent.

In 1997, there was a problem during a midterm exam in my Dis-covering Business class at San Jose State University. One student copied word for word (including several misspellings) the exam paper of the person sitting in the next seat. When I scheduled a meeting with them, they (a male and a female) stated they "always worked together" and felt I was wrong to call them in for a meeting. They were extremely upset when they discovered that I would give both of them an F for the class. After a very long meeting they still did not believe that there was an ethical issue in the situation. They stated that helping each other was not cheating. I still wonder what they will teach their children about cheating and ethics.

In the November 2002 edition of the newsletter for the Western Academy of Management, a short article on page five stated in part, "The results of the most recent Academy of Management Membership Survey suggest that many members are unfamiliar with the Code (of ethics) and have many concerns about how to apply and enforce it." This was the code of ethics for the group these people had joined.

On April 24, 2001, a University of California vice president of educational outreach (programs for underrepresented minorities) for the nine-campus UC system, Alex Saragoza, resigned. This resignation came in the wake of strong criticism of his giving credit to two football players attending the University of California at Berkeley campus for coursework they did not do. He had been a faculty member of the ethnic studies department at UC Berkeley since 1974. He gave passing grades in spring 1999 to these football players (who never attended classes) to allow them to remain eligible for the team. This situation came to light during the fall of 1999, yet it took almost two years for the vice president to resign. And the resignation only came after Berkeley's athletic program was put on probation for a year, resulting in the football team losing scholarships and the opportunity to play in a bowl game after the 2002 season. The most distressing part of the situation was that the *San Francisco Chronicle* wrote the next day (April 25, 2001) that UC president Richard Atkinson had not come to a conclusion over whether Saragoza should be asked to resign. UC spokesman Michael Reese said, "letters to Atkinson had been running about 50-50 pro and con" for a resignation. Fifty percent believed this behavior was ethical?

At Menlo College in Atherton, California, in 2002 there was a major ethical problem in the Professional Studies Program (for working adults). One of the professors was legally blind. The course evaluation form includes the question, "What is good about the instructor?" One student answered, "Can't see me while I am playing games on my phone." It seems that the classroom was really a playground. There are two issues here. First, the student had a very poor ethical standard and took advantage of the situation. Second, the student felt it was ethically OK to brag about this behavior.

Unfortunately, these are only a small sample of ethical problems today. Several books have been written about these examples, hundreds of newspaper articles, TV programs, and so on. I've just given a brief review of each example to demonstrate to the reader that ethics are a significant problem for negotiators in the twenty-first century. More could be included, but I believe the point has been made.

WORST POSSIBLE EXAMPLE

In February 2003, we discovered that my wife had inoperable cancer, and later she died. She started a protocol of strong chemotherapy that continued into the summer of 2003. In late July, I received a phone call. The person represented a dating service and said, "I understand that you are soon to be single and we want you to join our service [at a large fee] to find the right person for you." At that moment, I felt as if I had been hit in the gut by a Mack truck and I'm sure any reader in the same position would have the same feeling. This is the worst example of profit before compassion that I have ever seen, and an unethical negotiating position that I will never forget.

Savvy negotiators must remember that they are almost always in a position of negotiating the ground rules for a future relationship and are often representing another company or individual. Strong, productive win-win relationships do not evolve from unethical negotiations. I believe there are five lessons that savvy negotiators must always remember. This may not be the first time you have read these lessons—they are not new nor are they unique ideas—but they are keys to successful negotiations.

UNETHICAL NEGOTIATORS

The worst possible example leads into an important discussion concerning ethics. In negotiation courses and seminars, three of the most common questions are, "How can I spot an unethical negotiator?" "Is there a difference between an unethical negotiator and a manipulator?" "Is it ethical to use strategies and tactics in negotiations?" In this section, I address these three very significant issues in the negotiation process.

Addressing the first question and providing a foolproof answer is very difficult. There are many very successful con men (and women) who make a living using unethical techniques to take advantage of other people. Earlier in this chapter, I presented a number of examples of unethical behavior. Here's another to reinforce the point.

Most of us have heard of the "Nigerian letter." The letter claims that the writer has millions of dollars tied up in Nigeria. The writer explains that the money can be transferred to an American bank account. The total amount might be $50 million. If you give your bank account data, after the money is transferred to your account you will be able to keep $13 million. Many people have fallen for this trap and have given their bank account data, over e-mail, to the writer. The writer just clears out the account as soon as possible. I receive at least one such letter each week. Since each letter has a new sender, my junk mail screen doesn't catch the letter and it ends up in my in-box.

There are too many door-to-door selling scams to review here, but we must be very careful of them. Unethical negotiators use many of these techniques to gain your confidence in a deliberate effort to take advantage of you.

How to Identify Unethical Negotiators

Face-to-Face Negotiations

An important theme in this book is my very firm belief that the savvy negotiator will, whenever possible, negotiate in person. It has many advantages already discussed. Another advantage is that in face-to-face negotiations it is much easier to identify unethical negotiators. I list six reasons here.

First, nonverbal communications are one of the best ways to identify unethical people. First check out the eyes. As the poet says, "Eyes are the windows to the soul." I say the eyes are a great way to identify an unethical negotiator. Watch the blink rate. At the beginning of the negotiation, check out how many times your opponent blinks per minute (the average is eight to twelve, except for contact lens users, who blink more). When a person is under pressure, the blink rate will go way up. A major reason for pressure might be that the person is lying or is unethical. If the blink rate goes up, be very careful.

A September 1988 story in the *San Francisco Examiner* was titled "The Eyes Have It: What Blinking Says About the Candidates," by John Jacobs. In the article, he quoted Dr. Ralph Exline, a social psychologist at the University of Delaware, who counted the blinks during the televised debate between the candidates for president, George H. W. Bush and Michael Dukakis. Dukakis blinked about seventy times per minute and Bush blinked forty-three times per minute. The message to the voters was that Dukakis was uncomfortable, under pressure, and maybe not telling the truth. After the debate, the polls showed that Bush was ahead by a large margin, and Bush went on to win the election. The theme of the article was that the blink rate difference was a major factor in the viewer's perception of the two men.

At the other end of the spectrum is the person who is aware of the blink rate problem and stares at you. This is not natural. Every person has to blink. This is to keep the eyes moist, so the eyes will not be hurt. When a person does not blink, the person is probably lying or unethical.

Key to Success: Always Read the Eyes of Your Opponent

Second, other nonverbal messages include the following:

- Getting very close to you
- Being overly friendly
- Possible touching
- Using the open hand gesture, that is with palms up, fingers wide, showing that nothing is hidden, to "prove" honesty
- Talking softly, especially if others are in the area
- Keeping briefcase closed, to hide materials

Third, another sign of an unethical negotiator is the quick close. Why do negotiators try to close the deal quickly? If the deal was really fair, the negotiator would be happy to let you think about it and do some calculations. A fair deal can be tested. An unfair deal can't stand up to a test, so the unethical person wants to get a quick close (before you determine it is a bad deal for you).

Key to Success: Be Aware of the Quick Close

Fourth, remember that an unethical negotiator never gives without getting something of value. Unethical negotiators don't consider, or try to find out, your real needs. They tell you what your "needs" are and they have a deal to satisfy these needs.

Fifth, the negotiator exhibits a significant change in behavior from the past. The change usually indicates stress, which may be causing unethical behavior to remove the stress.

Sixth, unethical negotiators don't consider other options. They have a plan and stick to it no matter what. They may appear to be straightforward in their demand, offer, or position, but in fact they have no intention of actually negotiating a mutually beneficial outcome.

Written Negotiations

It is very hard to identify unethical negotiators in written negotiations. Savvy negotiators always keep their guard up and remember the very old (but still very true) adage: "There is no such thing as a free lunch." There is another old adage to remember: "If it seems too good to be true, it is too good to be true."

Key to Success: There Is No Free Lunch

Key to Success: If It Seems Too Good to Be True, It Is

Unless you are a Bill Gates, who can afford to give billions of dollars to charity every year, you don't just give stuff away. People and companies are motivated by their own self-interest. A company will not stay in business very long if they give away a lot of their product. Most of us know about the loss leader. That is, a company, using a newspaper advertisement, for example, will price a popular product below cost to get you to come into their store with the intent of selling you many other items at a higher-than- necessary price, which will generate a high per-unit profit. If they are successful, their total profit on your order will be high. Another unethical practice is the bait and switch. You are lured into a store to buy a certain item (for example, a two-door stripped-down Ford) at a good price. Once in the store, the salesperson will try to sell you a much higher-priced item at full price (for example, a Thunderbird with everything on it).

Key to Success: Be Aware of the Loss Leader

Key to Success: Be Aware of Bait-and-Switch Tactics

Manipulative Negotiators

The second common question is: "Is there a difference between an unethical negotiator and a manipulator?" First, a couple of definitions from *Merriam-Webster's Collegiate Dictionary*, Tenth Edition:

> manipulate (2) to control or play upon by artful, unfair or insidious means to one's own advantage (3) to change by artful or unfair means so as to serve one's purpose"
>
> insidious (1a) awaiting a chance to entrap (1b) harmful, but enticing

Why does a person use manipulative behavior? Weak people, or people with very weak negotiating leverage, may try to feel (be) stronger or to hide their weakness by using manipulative behavior. This is often the case—and the savvy negotiator does not fall into this trap. Strong people, or people with a strong position, may use their power just because they can. Both types of people do this to get their own way. Many times they just want to control the situation. They like to be in this position: "I have the power and there is nothing that you can do about it."

It seems to me that there is a difference, though often a subtle one, between unethical and manipulative negotiators. Here are a few examples of unethical or manipulative behavior.

1. A buyer wants his supplier to deliver exactly on the contract date, even thought the buyer knows that the material will not be needed for two months. The buyer just wants to prove that he is in control.
2. An artist wants the gallery to hang her pictures in a certain order (even though the gallery is very successful and knows the best way). If not, then

the artist wants the gallery to put more pictures on the Web site. The Web site and the way of hanging the pictures have nothing in common (apples and oranges). It is just that the artist wants to be in control.

3. A car salesperson sells a bad car to a very young couple who know nothing about cars or finances.

4. A woman promises sex to be able to go on a large shopping spree. Or a man promises sex to get money.

5. A parent promises an extra hour of TV that night if the child will finish all of her peas.

6. A person makes many last-minute schedule changes. For example, a team manager tells you on Friday that the soccer game on Saturday will be played at 9 a.m., not noon as originally scheduled. The manager knew this over a week before.

7. A girl comes into the kitchen where her grandmother is baking cookies. The grandmother keeps working and doesn't acknowledge her, although she is well aware of the granddaughter's presence. This goes on for fifteen minutes. Finally the grandmother says hello. When the granddaughter leaves, the grandmother expects (demands) hugs and kisses.

Which of the above examples are unethical and which are manipulative or just very poor negotiation practices? Write your answers down. My answers are at the end of this section.

A type of question that the savvy negotiator should be wary of is polling questions. People who conduct polls know that they can get any answer they want, based upon the wording of their questions. One example will prove this point.

Course Critique for an Industrial Training Course

1. Will you use techniques taught in this course?
2. How often will you use techniques taught in this course?

The first question is a yes-or-no question, and many students could answer no. That would indicate that the course was not very valuable. The second question will get some kind of number from every student, "proving" that the course is valuable. Which question do you think the course manager will use—especially if the manager's boss asks, "How did the course go?"

The very best example of manipulative behavior is one that all parents and grandparents can relate to. A little kid comes into a room where both of the kid's parents are sitting. The little kid looks at Mommy, reading her current nonverbal communications. Then the little kid looks at Daddy, again reading nonverbal communications. Then the kid goes to one of the parents and says, "Can I have X?" Of course that parent says yes.

From the above discussion, the reader should understand that manipulative people are really conducting one-way negotiations. Both sides may communicate, but one side has control and wants to achieve their objectives at the expense of the other side.

Strategies and Tactics

First, two definitions, again from *Merriam-Webster's Collegiate Dictionary*:

strategy (2A) a careful plan or method (2b) the art of devising or employing plans or stratagems toward a goal

tactics (1b) the art or skill of employing available means to accomplish an end

There are several viewpoints concerning strategies and tactics in negotiations. I very strongly believe that 99.999 percent of negotiators have a planned strategy before they enter into a negotiation. All of these people believe that it is very ethical to prepare strategies before every negotiation. Every negotiator that I have ever talked to was convinced that a requirement of being a negotiator is to have a well-prepared strategy before every negotiation. I agree with them. It is ethical to prepare your negotiation before you negotiate.

Tactics are another issue, because there are so many different tactics. Several books have been completely devoted to reviewing negotiation tactics in great detail. There are very unethical tactics, very manipulative tactics, and very acceptable tactics. I urge you to purchase a couple of these books (for example, *Give and Take* by Karrass and *Negotiation Strategies for Mutual Gain* by Hall) so you can identify tactics when they are used against you. Then you will not be pushed into a bad agreement. The savvy negotiator is fully aware of all negotiation tactics. I have a very firm belief that it is best to be upfront with your opponent. We don't want to play games with people with whom we are establishing the ground rules for our future relationship. This is especially true if this relationship is aimed at satisfying our needs.

Hints to Remember

To review this section, the savvy negotiator must remember these keys concerning an opponent's unethical or manipulative behaviors:

1. There is no such thing as a free lunch.
2. If it seems to good to be true, it is.

Remember that the savvy person negotiates to set the ground rules for a future relationship. Successful relationships happen when both sides have their needs met. Beware of proposed deals in which you come out way ahead. Also beware of deals that are barely lawful. Any deal that is on the edge of being illegal probably is really over the edge and breaks the law. If the deal is so great, why isn't everyone in on it?

3. Beware the loss leader.
4. Beware the bait and switch.

We all have heard of these practices many times in the past. All too often we forget, because the offer looks like just what we want.

5. Continue to explore other options. Ask many "what if" questions.
6. Unethical negotiators never give without getting, and most of the time they get more.
7. Always test the logic of the other side's position. If the logic is too perfect, be careful. If the logic is too imperfect, also be careful.
8. Unethical negotiators always want to have the last word.
9. Unethical negotiators must always prove they are in control.

In conclusion to this section, I raise a fourth question that is frequently asked by students in negotiation courses and seminars: "Are ethics in negotiations different than ethics in the rest of my life?" If anyone says yes, they have flunked the course. When you enter a negotiation, whether it is in a formal negotiation room, in your own home, on the street, or at a garage sale, never leave your ethics at the door.

Earlier in this section, there was a small quiz. I believe that the an-swers (unethical or manipulative) are based on the intent of the other side. Here are my answers:

1. Manipulative
2. Manipulative
3. Unethical
4. Unethical
5. Manipulative
6. Manipulative
7. Manipulative

This section can be summarized with two important points. First, the savvy negotiator is constantly on guard against unethical or manipula-tive opponents. By often referring to this book, and specifically this chap-ter, you will be able to keep your guard up. Second, the savvy negotiator knows that negotiation is the best option to resolve conflicts and formalize agreements. All of the other options are win-lose options. Both sides must work to satisfy needs and to have an agreement that benefits both sides. Again, we negotiate to set the ground rules for a future relationship and we want that relationship to be a win-win relationship. Savvy negotiators will influence and manage negotiations; they will never manipulate ne-gotiations. Savvy negotiators are ethical in all of their actions.

LESSONS FOR SAVVY NEGOTIATORS

1. *Put your integrity first.* Finding unique loopholes in the law may make a certain action legal, but this doesn't make it right. Finding a way around a reporting requirement may make you look good in the short term, but it doesn't make for a business that lasts for several decades.

2. *Don't take the first (small) step.* At Susquehanna University in Se-linsgrove, Pennsylvania, Richard Davis teaches business law classes. White-collar criminals from a nearby prison are allowed to visit his clas-ses and lecture to his students. Their message is: Stay away from the gray areas, from people who operate on the fringes, and from small ethical mis-steps that lead to larger ones. Very few people make their first ethical mistake a major mistake. But after making many small and medium-sized mistakes, a large one doesn't seem that large anymore.

3. *Understand the overall picture.* It is important to understand your potential actions in the overall picture, not just in this month's results. Take personal responsibility for your actions and be sure you understand all the implications of every action you take in every negotiation you are involved in, business or personal, large or small, individual or team.

4. *Have the courage to speak out.* It is very important that you have the courage to speak out and ask questions when a potential ethical problem situation occurs. If you are in a management position, always be open to your employees and never ignore or retaliate against legitimate concerns.

5. *Good honest business practices always beat short-term profits.* This lesson is that no possible short-term success is important enough to be achieved at the price of illegal, dishonest, or unethical practices. Doing business the right way is the only way to do business.

6. *Your actions are either right or wrong.* It is not that simple with ethics. There are many situations that are not really clear-cut. Before making a decision, the savvy negotiator will get all important facts about the situation.

7. *People usually do things right.* We are not born with an ethical standard. Ethics is a learned behavior. You must continually work at being ethical.

8. *Good people don't behave unethically.* No one is perfect. Just because a person has been "good" all her life doesn't mean that in any specific situation she will automatically do the right thing.

9. *I have to do what my principle tells me to do.* This is a very bad mistake to make. We have too many examples today of individuals getting into trouble because they did what they were told. Today this is NO DEFENSE for your actions. I have turned down opportunities to negotiate for companies that asked me to lie at the negotiation table. I was told, "If you are caught, we'll just tell the other side that we didn't give you the data. That way you (Bill Morrison) will be off the hook. If the other side doesn't catch you, our side will be ahead in the negotiation."

10. *It is better to ask for forgiveness than to ask for permission.* This may be true when making some management decisions, but it is never true when making ethical decisions.

FINAL CONSIDERATIONS

Whenever you are faced with an uncomfortable situation in your business or personal life, especially in negotiations that could have ethical implications, ask yourself these five questions before you act:

1. Is this action OK with my company or my organization?
   Is it legal?
   Does it meet company or organization policy?
   Will it hurt my boss if it comes to light?
   Can I put this action on my resume?
2. Is it OK with my profession?
   Every important position has a professional organization for people doing that work. For example, the American Production and Inventory Control Society (APICS) is for people who work in inventory control, production control, and materials and supply chain management positions. Each professional organization has a code of ethics. The purpose of this second question is for you to check the code of ethics for your profession before taking action.
3. Is it OK with my culture?
   Every culture has behaviors that are acceptable and behaviors that are unacceptable. Many are written, and many are not, but all have been accepted by a large majority of the population and have become norms for behavior. Unacceptable behaviors in negotiations in any culture will make it very difficult for the negotiator to obtain a true win-win result and have acceptable ground rules for a future relationship. So, if your answer to this question is no, how can the relationship established via the negotiation process be a solid relationship?
4. Is it OK with my family?
   After I complete this action, can I call my spouse, my children, or my grandchildren and brag about what I just did? Can I tell them that they should do in the future what I just did? If I can't advise my family to follow my behavior, the behavior is probably wrong.
5. Finally, is it OK with me?
   Each reader must live with himself.

In my classes at San Jose State University when I review ethics, I discuss the "Morrison Mirror Test." I suggest that the day each person retires, they will have to go into the bathroom before they leave for their job. They will look into the mirror and have to ask themselves several questions. "Am I proud of the way I behaved during my career?" "Was my behavior a good example for my family, my peers, and my organization?" "Will others follow in my path?"

At that time, they might be able to lie to their families about how they feel. They might be able to lie to their friends and neighbors. They might be able to lie to their peers at work. They might even be able to lie to their boss. But they will not be able to lie to themselves. Inside themselves they will know the truth. On retirement day it is too late to change the ethical score, and each of us must live with that score for the rest of our lives.

Key to Success: Take the Morrison Mirror Test When You Retire

Then in my classes I draw this comparison: "Here at San Jose State we give many quizzes in order to prepare students to take and do well on the final exam. If you want to pass the final exam of your career, you must take a weekly ethical quiz." I urge the students to take a weekly Morrison Mirror Quiz. Each Monday before you start a new week, look yourself in the face and ask, "Am I proud of the way I behaved last week? Can I brag about my behavior?" If the answer is yes each week, you will pass the final exam with flying colors. If the answer is no, you will have time to correct your behavior.

Key to Success: Pass the Morrison Mirror Quiz Each Week

Ethics is emphasized in every class I teach at both the graduate and undergraduate levels, in every seminar I conduct for companies, in every public seminar I'm asked to be part of, and in every public speech I give. I have a very strong belief in ethical behavior by all people, especially negotiators, who are establishing ground rules for future relationships, and I preach this philosophy at every opportunity I get.

This is a short chapter, but a very important one. I believe it is one of the most important keys to success in all your negotiations and in all your other future relationships.

Key to Success: Ethical Behavior Is a Must in All Negotiations

II
Winning Your Day-to-Day Negotiations

CHAPTER 5

Day-to-Day Negotiation Situations

In part I, many of the examples came from the business world. Such negotiations are generally high-value negotiations that start a long-term corporate relationship. They are the ones we often hear about on TV or read about in the daily newspaper. Readers can relate to these, because they all know a lot about them. Some readers may even have been directly involved. The point is that most of us are aware of these negotiations. Many times the key points are easier to see and understand when they come from big negotiations that are in the public domain.

In our business lives, many of us are called upon to negotiate in buyer-seller negotiations, in management-labor negotiations, or within our company with other people or departments. We see the negotiation process as an important part of our business lives. We accept this fact and we do the best we can in each negotiation situation. We know that successful negotiations can have a major impact of the success of our organization.

In my first book, I proved that a 1 percent better negotiations job by the buyers in a company and a 1 percent better negotiations job by the sellers in a company will result in a 20–35 percent increase in profits after tax for that company. This significant impact is the reason that so many companies conduct negotiation training courses and workshops for their key people. In business, there is a significant return on investment for negotiation training courses.

There is another area of our lives, our personal lives, where negotiations can also have a significant impact. Almost every day, each one of us is part of a negotiation that is outside of our business or professional responsibilities. Whether we like it or not, negotiations are part of twenty-first-century culture. It is a fact that negotiations are part of life. Outside of business, these generally are small or smaller negotiations, but the outcome will certainly influence our happiness and many times affect our wealth. The financial impact may mean more to us as individuals than to an organization. Especially important are family negotiations that may not involve any money, but certainly have a major impact on our happiness and the happiness of the important people in our lives.

I cannot understand a person who preaches a win-win philosophy at work and then displays win-lose behavior at home. We have accepted that negotiations set the ground rules for a future relationship and that the objective must be a win-win outcome for each negotiation. How can anyone play win-lose with the most important people in their life? I believe that a major reason for the very high divorce rate, especially in the United States, is that many family negotiations are win-lose negotiations.

This part of the book is aimed at helping every person win these small but very important negotiations. The key concepts in chapter 2 apply to all negotiations, so keep these concepts in mind when involved in a small or day-to-day negotiation. The key question and answer techniques in chapter 3 also apply to our day-to-day negotiations, so these techniques must be remembered. And we cannot forget the ethics lessons in chapter 4.

I emphasize that almost everything is negotiable (remember in chapter 2, I reviewed the "ask-for" concept). Many people, especially in the United States, believe that with the exception of houses and cars, anything with a price tag is not negotiable. This is not true. Most big-ticket items such as appliances, furniture, and travel are always negotiable. Many small-ticket items are always open to negotiation in department stores, specialty stores, and mall stores. So I urge the reader to try negotiations whenever possible. It is more difficult to negotiate in grocery stores, but even there, if you are buying a large quantity, you should ask for a better price.

Just a few examples will prove this point. First, the May 4, 2003, edition of the *San Jose Mercury News* (on the first page of the business section) carried an article titled "Haggling for Bargains." The article reported, "A survey of 1000 consumers found the point at which most felt comfortable asking for a discount is $200–down from $500 in 1990." The article listed many items that are often negotiated such as major household appliances, electronics, clothes, taxicab and limousine rides, and furniture. This indicates that if you ask for a discount on purchases at $200 or above, you are in the majority, and this should not be a surprise to the store or the store's personnel.

A second example from the *Mercury News* comes from an article about a local jewelry chain that discussed the fact that each piece of jewelry had three prices. This article stated, "Most salespeople will offer the middle price, but according to insiders, repeat customers who come in and declare they wouldn't shop anywhere but Shane's usually get nailed with the highest price." A good lesson is that you must negotiate even if you are a good customer of that store.

Third, the November 16, 2001, issue of the *Wall Street Journal* contained an article titled "A Haggler's Christmas" that discussed the new negotiation environment and stated, "From small boutiques to Saks Fifth Avenue a surprising array of stores are starting to let consumers bargain over prices." Twelve stores across the United States were specifically mentioned, including the Disney Store and Eddie Bauer Home. Today, almost every store will bargain. The authors of that article suggested that buyers always start with the question, "Is this your best price?"

A fourth example is another *Journal* article that asked, "Did you overpay for your car?" It reviewed many areas in which dealers add unwanted or unneeded extras to a car, many times without the buyer's knowledge.

A final and interesting example comes from professional basketball. A few years ago, Jerry Stackhouse was about to become a free agent. He stated, "It's not necessarily what you do [on the basketball court] in your three years [before becoming a free agent], it's what your representatives do when they sit in front of the suits and ties [owners]." His message is that his agent's negotiation skills could get him a lot more money than his basketball skills.

I could write a whole book with similar examples that prove many people are negotiating personal items every day. I have files full of articles similar to the five reviewed above. People who just accept the price and don't try to save money are not only paying too much, but they are in effect subsidizing the people who do negotiate. Yes, subsidizing! Consider this example: a store wants to receive an average price of $10 for an item and puts a price tag of $11 on the item. For every item that the store sells at $11 (to nonnegotiating buyers), it can afford to sell as low as $9 to a buyer who really negotiates. The store gets both sales and the average price the store needs to make a profit.

The basis for part II has been evolving for many years. For over forty years in almost every one of the several of hundreds of negotiation training programs that I have presented, someone has made an important comment that generally goes like this: "This is great information if you are in a large industrial or not-for-profit negotiation, but it will not help me because all I do is negotiate small items for my company or just personal items for myself." Sometimes others add, "Many of my negotiations are on the phone or the Internet, so the nonverbal communications techniques you taught us are really of very little use."

The more I heard these comments, the more I knew that additional material must be presented in these training programs. Since 1995, I've spent several hours on four new subjects in each course: small negotiations, day-to-day negotiations, telephone negotiations, and Internet and written negotiations.

Also, the more I heard these comments, the more I became convinced that a section of a book devoted to day-to-day negotiation would be useful, not only to these students but also to other people. It became very clear that a significant need existed and this is the reason for this section of the book.

The major focus in part II is on smaller day-to-day negotiations. My research has shown that there are several keys to winning our day-to-day negotiations. We must always understand the process of negotiation and understand the key concepts that provide success in big negotiations, business negotiations, personal negotiations, and day-to-day negotiations. These are givens. Several other concepts are especially useful in the reader's smaller negotiations, and these concepts are reviewed in part II.

As you read part II, please remember the core of this book is the Keys to Success that appear in every chapter. These form the basic learning objectives for this book. You will find many new keys in this section. Remember, they are truly your keys to success in all your future negotiations.

You must understand that all of the principles discussed in the first four chapters are important to being a savvy negotiator in your day-to-day negotiations. These will apply to all your negotiations and should guide your behavior in the new century. An understanding of the twenty-first-century model of negotiations can help you be successful in all your negotiations, especially the day-to-day ones.

For interest and organization, I have broken the day-to-day negotiations into six categories:

PRIMARILY MONEY
1. Work situations
2. Home purchase negotiations
3. Buying or selling autos
4. Travel negotiations

PRIMARILY NOT MONEY
5. Family negotiations
6. Other negotiations

The two key purposes of part II are to help you identify situations that should be considered for a negotiation and to help you achieve significantly more successful outcomes in these day-to-day negotiations.

Each category of negotiation uses the same outline. Several examples of actual negotiations are reviewed to demonstrate the wide range of potential negotiation situations in our day-to-day lives. To prove there are thousands of opportunities in our daily lives, I list a large number of situations that call for a negotiation. The list may seem long and you may say, "Why list so many? I get the picture." The reason is to make such a large impression that you will be motivated to start negotiating at the first opportunity. Please remember: the list is not all-inclusive.

After the six categories are reviewed, this chapter closes with several hints on how to be more successful in all your general day-to-day negotiations. The hints apply to almost all situations. Many are self-evident. All are important.

For many years, I have required each student in my university negotiation and conflict resolution classes (both undergraduate and graduate level) to write about a recent real-world negotiation in which the student was involved. The student did not have to have done well in the negotiation or even have completed it, just be an important part of it. As a result, I have literally thousands of examples of day-to-day negotiations. Some of them are humorous, but all are real. For legal and ethical reasons, names are not given. But please be assured that I did not change the heart of any of the students' reports.

WORK SITUATIONS

It is impossible to share all the details of all the work situations that I have in my file. It seems that this area takes the greatest amount of negotiation time for many of my students, peers, and friends. During the first class session of my university classes, the students fill in an interest form that says, "Rank the most important negotiations you are or will be involved in." The negotiation situation that always ranks first is negotiating with my boss, especially for a raise. Here is a short list of the subjects and situations that should always be considered negotiable in work situations:

1. Job/salary related
   A. Interviewing: entry level (no experience)
      Intern
      Reentry to work force
      Promotion in current company
      Position in new company
   B. Job offers
   C. Job responsibilities
   D. Salary and salary increases
   E. Performance reviews
   F. Job-sharing arrangements
   G. Work shifts
   H. Workers' compensation
   I. Disability accommodations
   J. Benefits—medical and dental
   K. Retirement—regular, 401K, other
   L. Job for spouse as part of a move
   M. Vacation
   N. Flextime
   O. Time for family problems (illness, etc.)
   P. Substance abuse and support programs
   Q. Legal support system
   R. Training and development courses
   S. Higher education rebates
   T. Working conditions
   U. Resources to complete responsibilities
2. Management–Labor
3. Boss–Subordinate
4. Peer–Peer

5. Allocation of departmental resources
6. Schedule issues
7. Meetings
8. Customers
9. Suppliers
10. Government agencies

The key to most business negotiations is the bottom line. You've noticed that in annual reports, after the up-front public relations information, the back end is all numbers. We must always focus on the bottom line. This is a must in the twenty-first century. When I joined the Westinghouse Electric Corp. in 1957, almost everyone in business expected hiring decisions to be lifetime decisions. That is, I expected that if Westinghouse treated me fairly, I would stay at Westinghouse for my full career. Westinghouse expected that if I completed my responsibilities and met or exceeded my objectives, they would keep me for my full career. This would be a pact or a "contract" even if the business didn't do too well for a short time period. At that time, business measurements were based on a longer term than today's measurements. Management would make an investment in their human resources by keeping many people in a down market. Management also did more to develop people through more management and technical courses, lateral assignments, and developmental assignments. In the twenty-first century, three months is long term, lifetime employment no longer available, and the stock price drives many businesses. So today the first thing we think about in business negotiations is the bottom line.

When a company representative is interviewing a possible hire, the representative wants to determine if this person will be able to make the representative look good. In 99.9 percent of the cases, this means make the company look good. Will this person contribute to the company or organization? Applicants are selling themselves to the company. (The resume is the advertisement and the interview is the sale.) The very best way to convince people that you will make them look good is if you made your last boss look good. The secret to winning a new job is to have a long list of your accomplishments (very measurable and objective) from your previous jobs. It is easy to sell a product (yourself, in interviews) if the product was excellent in the past.

This attitude is also the key to getting a raise at your current job. Too many people focus on the time since the last raise and say; "I'm due for a raise." Others focus on the need for a raise such as a new child, medical problems, inflation, new home, and so on. These are not reasons for a raise. To be more successful in receiving a raise, you must focus on your accomplishments (especially those that support section, department, and company goals). You must make the case that based on your specific accomplishments, you have been underpaid and you have earned a raise. The company should (must) raise your pay or promote you to a level of pay that equals your accomplishments.

Key to Success: Focus on Real, Provable Accomplishments

Each worker must keep an accomplishment file; some call it a brag file. Every time you get a complimentary letter, put it in your brag file. If you have success without a letter, make a note and put it in the brag file. If you make a suggestion to your boss, a peer, or top management that is implemented and improves productivity or profit, make a note and put it in your brag file. If you do something that improves customer or supplier relations, make a note and put it in your brag file. If you do some thing in your community that improves your company's image, make a note and put it in your brag file. If you have completed a training course or received a college degree, make a note and put it in your brag file. Everything must be saved. It is very easy to forget accomplishments from a year ago (or longer) if you have not documented them in the daily rush of business. These accomplishments will be the key to a raise or promotion. It is a great feeling to go to a merit review meeting with your boss armed with a long list of actual and provable accomplishments that have had an impact on your company's bottom line.

Key to Success: Keep a Detailed Brag File for Raise and Promotion Negotiations

---

An important key is the ask-for concept. The company will never give you more than you ask for. If your company was planning to give you a

7 percent raise and you ask for a 5 percent raise, the company will be very happy to meet your requirement (and save 2 percent at the same time). Or the company will make you very happy by giving you a 5.2 percent raise that is above your request.

When negotiating with others in your company for resources (third on the interest list), the key is company goals. You must prove that your project, department, group, or what have you needs the resources more, because if you don't get the resources, a major company goal will be missed.

Outside of these situations, there are a great many negotiation opportunities in business. The most common are buyer-seller, union-management, and customer service negotiations. Several fine books cover these negotiations in great depth. On the form listing the types of negotiations they are most interested in, the second most listed type is negotiating with the student's spouse, children, or boyfriend/girlfriend. These are listed before auto, home, appliances, and so on.

HOME PURCHASE NEGOTIATIONS

Negotiating to buy your home is very difficult because purchasing a home has a very strong emotional component. This emotional component is generally much stronger than in almost every other negotiation that we are a part of. An important key to success is to keep all emotions out of home negotiations. You must get all the facts before you negotiate. With a lot of information, facts, and numbers to guide you, you should be able to have better control of your emotions. All experts agree that buyers must be preapproved for a loan, so buyers know their limits and don't offer too much. Other points the experts agree on are that the buyer must know the history of the house for the last several years, how long the house has been on the market, if the seller purchased another house, and if there are potential competing offers.

A perfect example of how emotions influence the real estate process occurred when I purchased a home in the Pittsburgh area. The town of Mt. Lebanon had an outstanding school system, and I was absolutely committed to living there. We found the perfect house. An elderly woman who had lived in the house for most for her life was the seller. Now a widow, she was moving to Florida. She had set a very high asking price. In private, her real estate agent told that the house was highly overpriced, but that was what the owner wanted so that was what the agent was asking. The next day I was in the house and the owner showed me to a point in the living room and said, "This is the exact spot where my first grandchild took his first step." Now I knew why the owner was asking such a high price. The house had a very high emotional value to the owner. The negotiations took several months before the owner was convinced by her agent, her kids, and the lack of other offers to accept our offer, which reflected the home's true market value.

Key to Success: Keep Emotions Out of Home Purchase Negotiations

---

Another factor that has a major impact on price is the nature of current market conditions: buyers' market or sellers' market. To illustrate this point, two homes next to each other, built at the same time, sold on my street in Palo Alto, California, for a huge difference in price. One sold for $1.3 million (asking price was $899,000) at the very height of the housing boom related to the business boom and soaring dot.com era in the late 1990s and very early 2000s. The other sold for $700,000 about two years later, and this house had a pool and more land than the house that sold earlier.

When I moved to California in the mid-1980s, it was a normal market, so I was able to take a few weeks to find the right house. The final negotiation was between my agent and the owner and the owner's agent. I waited in my car outside the house reading a book while the negotiations were conducted. I did not want to be part of the negotiation because I might have signaled (without being aware of it) that I really wanted the house. With that information, the owner might have held out for a higher price. I took emotions out of the negotiation and let my agent negotiate using facts. I got the house at a fair price based on the time of the negotiation and the location of the house.

Key to Success: Location and Market Timing Are Critical to the Final Price

---

In the *New York Times Magazine* dated August 3, 2002, there was an article titled, "The Probability That a Real-Estate Agent Is Cheating

You (and Other Riddles of Modern Life)." The author, Stephen J. Dubner, wrote about the "heralded young economist" Steven Levitt and some of Levitt's studies, papers, and opinions. Levitt took up the hobby of buying, remodeling, and selling old houses in the town he lived in, Oak Park, Illinois. He found that many times, the seller's agent would encourage him to always bid, and even to underbid. Levitt wondered why. "The key, Levitt determined, lay in the fact the agents 'receive only a small share of incremental profit when a house sells for a higher value.' Like a stock-broker churning commissions, or a bookie grabbing his vig, an agent was simply looking to make a deal, any deal."

Another key part of this article is this: in his study of more than 50,000 home sales in Cook County, Levitt found that homes owned by real estate agents stayed on the market about ten days longer and sold for 2 percent more. These agents understood that they could put extra money in their pockets by waiting for a better deal. The point for each of us to remember is the agent will generally put the agent's interests first, so when you are buying or selling a home, be careful of an agent who wants to make a quick sale.

When you are looking for an agent, there are several things to consider. Buyers want an agent who has done all the preplanning and prep work. Sellers want an agent who works full time and really knows the area. Always interview several agents before you sign a contract and look for the characteristics that the best agents have in common:

1. Person is a licensed realtor (not just a salesperson or a broker)
2. Works full time in the area where you are looking
3. Is easy to get in touch with
4. Has an experienced support team in the office
5. Has several years' experience in this business
6. Reputation (ask for names of clients from the past six months and contact them for references)

During your interview, try to determine if the agent has these characteristics:

7. Has a process for decision making
8. Negotiation skills
9. Communication skills
10. Ethics, ethics, ethics

Stay away from agents who:

1. Have too many listings (ten to twelve should be the maximum)
2. Tell you they can guarantee your price (just to get a contract). No one can guarantee a price unless it is way out of line.
3. Don't know the area
4. Brag too much about past successes (those sales may have occurred during a very different market)
5. You don't comfortable with as people

Always be aware of the agent's true objectives.

One of my students almost learned a hard lesson at the cost of $30,000. He and his wife were renting a three-bedroom starter home when they learned that the woman who owned the house had decided to sell. They had told her earlier that they would like to have the first opportunity to buy. They had had a good relationship during the rental period and in fact did receive an opportunity to buy before the house was listed.

When they were notified that the owner wanted to sell, but before they met with the real estate agent, they did some fact finding. They found that real estate prices had dropped over the preceding few years, but that no comparable houses had sold in the immediate area in the last year. During the first meeting with the real estate agent, the agent was unable to show any actual sales but stated that the owner was asking a fair price of $275,000. My student asked that a certified appraiser complete an appraisal. The agent picked an appraiser (whom the agent had worked with for many years) who appraised the property at just a few thousand dollars less than the asking price. The buyers did not believe that they could qualify for a loan big enough to buy the house at the appraised price, but they really wanted the house. They decided to make an offer to buy at the asking price contingent on the lender appraising the house at that value and approving my student and his wife for the loan. This strategy would keep the house off the open market for a few more days. In the meantime, my student got preapproved for a loan at a local bank.

A week later, the real estate agent called to say that the owner had accepted the offer, and a meeting was arranged at the bank. The bank stated that it was their policy to always have their own appraisal before approving a loan. Their appraiser determined that the house was only worth $245,000 and the loan was turned down. The real estate agent stated that the buyers would have to make up the $30,000 difference in cash.

The buyers stated that the bank had a much better idea of the true market value of the house and they were going to make an offer at the bank's appraised price. They truly believed that this would be a very fair price for both the buyer and the seller. The real estate agent first refused to give the offer to the seller. Finally the agent told them she would give the offer to the seller, but she would strongly recommend that the seller reject the offer.

The seller accepted the offer, the loan was approved, my student and his wife owned their first home, and the seller was pleased with her significant profit. This was a win-win because both sides accepted a price that was determined by an objective third party.

Key to Success: Understand the Agent's True Objectives

What are the key objectives for any real estate agent? One, sell the house as quickly as possible, because time is money. Two, sell the house as quickly as possible, because time is money. Three, sell at the highest possible price (because the higher the price, the higher the commission), but not at the cost of time. Remember the Levitt example. Agents can be extremely helpful when buying or selling a home, and I know of many who are excellent in their jobs. However, you must always be on guard to protect your interests.

A friend of mine who worked with me at a Westinghouse Electric Corporation plant in Sunnyvale, California, had a similar experience. He owned a lot on the Olympic Peninsula in the state of Washington. The lot next to his went on sale for $22,000 and he decided to buy it. My friend checked the recent sales records at the courthouse and found that the value for that size lot was $12,000. He told the real estate agent to give the buyer an offer of $10,000. (This was an initial position and my friend expected to go up to $12,000 or $13,000.) The agent refused. My friend asked two more times and both times the agent refused. My friend called the owner directly and said, "Your agent refused to give you my offer, so I'm calling you. Based upon the county records, I feel a fair price is $10,000. I am now making a firm offer of $10,000. I can give you a check tomorrow for that amount." The owner was very upset at her agent and said she would call my friend back. The owner then fired the real estate agent. Next the owner called my friend and accepted the offer, if my friend paid for the transfer taxes ($500). The lot was sold and both sides were happy. The agent was not happy because the owner never paid any commission to the agent. But this was the agent's fault, because the agent refused to present the offer to the owner.

Listed in chapter 9 of my first book, *The Pre-Negotiation Planning Book*, are several issues to be considered when buying or selling a house. Too often buyers and sellers only focus on price and forget the many other key parts of a house purchase. A few of the most important are listed below for your future reference.

Positive Issues	Negative Issues
Neighborhood	Empty lot nearby
Good schools	Under airplane path
Good school district	Neighborhood association
Good weather in that specific neighborhood	High noise levels
	Bad views
Quiet streets	Near freeways
Easy to get to work	Commercial property nearby
Easy to find entertainment	Toxic chemical area
Close to shopping areas	Regional development plans
High water quality	Easements (third party)
Public transportation	Near major power lines
Low utility costs	Near railroad lines
Newer appliances	High-crime-rate area
New roof	Sex offender in area
Low tax rates	In flood zone
Good zoning rules	Bad zoning rules
Resale value	Cost of insurance
Smallest home in area	Largest home in area
Room sizes	Potential unacceptable views
Good lot size	On or near a busy street

Key to Success: Negotiate All Issues When Buying or Selling a Home

A home's location is critical. Everything about the home can be changed (color, appliances, etc.), but not the location and what is nearby. Another critical factor is which side (buyer or seller) pays the many sales expenses and taxes. In my book, forty-three different taxes and fees and many prepurchase inspections are listed. Each one must be negotiated.

A very good friend in the real estate business offered the following nuggets of advice.

For buyers, if your offer to buy is rejected, don't be shy about finding out why. There may be several reasons: (1) there were competing offers and your offer was too low; (2) you had too many contingencies in your offer; (3) the seller had an unrealistic price; or (4) something happened in the seller's life that distracted the seller. Each of these reasons should be a learning lesson for the buyer. Also be sure to check the permit history of the home to determine if any remodeling was done without the required permits.

If you have young children, buying in an area where there are very good schools usually is a good decision. There are two options: first, buy in an area with average schools (paying a lower price) and send your children to a private school, or, second, buy in an area with high-quality schools (paying a higher price) and send them to the public school. Many experts recommend the second option. Your children will receive a very good education and you will have a higher net worth.

For sellers, in a normal market, it is to the seller's advantage to play a waiting game. The longer the house is on the market and the more people see the house, the more offers will be made. The seller has to make a choice of one of two procedures: the seller can listen to any bid when a potential buyer makes one or the seller can set a day and time for a bid opening. The advantage for a bid opening is that potential buyers will assume there will be many offers and the buyer may bid at a higher price. In general, buyers want to get into their new home as soon as possible and they generally have a more urgent need for the sale to be completed.

Finally, you should consider whether to buy, build, or rent. There are advantages to each one, and all options must considered before a final decision is made. Most people involved in the housing business would agree with the following three basic lists.

Reasons to Buy

1. You plan to stay in that house for at least four years.
2. You have a high confidence level that you will be employed and have a secure income for the next several years.
3. You have the resources (time and money) to complete all required home maintenance and repairs. If you defer maintenance, you will generally get a lower price when you sell.
4. You can pay the monthly mortgage payments (principal and interest) plus insurance and taxes.
5. You are able to see the purchase as a long-term investment.
6. You understand (and accept) that you might be able to rent a larger house, but you want to own.
7. You have considered the potential resale value and planned an exit strategy.

Reasons to Rent

1. You do not plan to stay in the area for at least four years.
2. You get bored easily and want the flexibility to move when you want to move.
3. You do not have the important skills or resources to maintain your home.
4. You are not in a secure job position.
5. You have required fixed payments that are a large percentage of your total income.
6. You do not have sufficient cash flow to pay the monthly payments.
7. You want to budget your money for travel and other entertainment activities.

Reasons to Build

1. You expect to be in the area for a long time and want to customize your home (remembering that this may make it harder to sell).
2. You have strong negotiation skills to be able to negotiate a fair deal with the builder.
3. You have the time to conduct many formal and detailed contractor interviews to get the best. Research shows that many people are too soft when dealing with potential contractors. Be sure to ask lots of questions (see chapter 3). A good contract ensures a good relationship. A key is a detailed scope of work.
4. You have unique needs.
5. You want the opportunity to pick your colors and all other inside choices.

In our personal lives, the home purchase or sale negotiation is the most important money negotiation we face, and each person must work very hard to ensure a successful negotiation.

AUTO NEGOTIATIONS

Three major types of negotiations are included when we think of auto negotiations: buying a car, car repairs, and insurance claims. Since buying a car involves the most money, there are several hints to improve your buying skills in this section.

A friend who had been very successful selling cars for many years before he retired gave me an important lesson in buying a car when he said, "I call the list price for a car the stupid price. Anyone who pays list price is either stupid, lazy, or extremely rich." He also said, "We make a lot of money when we complicate the deal, especially when a trade-in is involved. What we do is keep changing the numbers on both the new car and the trade-in, so the buyer loses track of the true cost of the new car. Many times I've been able to make a larger profit by reducing the value of a 'good deal' on a new car by making a bad deal on the trade-in. This is added profit for the dealer and more commission for me."

What I learned from this veteran was to negotiate the best deal for the new car first and get a firm, written quote, then negotiate the trade-in. What really counts is how much money goes with the deal. When you buy a car, generally you give the dealer the keys to your old car (trade-in) and money. Since you are giving up the old car anyway, the only thing that counts is the amount of money that goes with the deal.

The dealer negotiates in two ways. First, if the buyer thinks he or she is a real negotiator, the dealer will give a good discount on the new car, but give a low value for the trade-in. For example, the list price for the new car is $32,000. The dealer reduces the price to $27,000 but only allows $5,000 for the trade-in. Second, if the buyer believes the trade-in is in perfect shape, the dealer will give a higher value for that trade-in and only give a small discount for the new car. Using the same example of a list price of $32,000, the dealer gives a value for the trade-in of $8,000 with a firm price for the new car of $30,000.

In the first example, the buyer had to pay $22,000 for the new car (price of $27,000 minus trade-in of $5,000). In the second example, the buyer had to pay $22,000 for the new car (price of $30,000 minus trade-in of $8,000). Both buyers were happy as they made their objective. The dealer was really happy, because the dealer made a big profit. Always keep your eye on the money that goes with the deal.

There are several sales tactics that each buyer must be aware of and understand to be a successful car buyer. A few examples follow.

Negative Concession

The first time you visit a dealer, you get a value for your trade-in. When you return to seriously negotiate a deal, the dealer asks for the keys to your trade-in so his service department can make a detailed inspection. During your first visit, the dealer's trade-in value for your car was based upon his knowledge of the market at that time. Only if there is a major question at the dealer's will the service department really give the car a detailed inspection. Many trade-in cars go straight to an auction, so there is no need for the service department to spend a lot of time on the car. The real objective of asking for the keys is so that you cannot leave the dealership. When you are ready to leave, the salesperson will call the service department to get your keys. You might be told that the person who has the keys is taking another car to get gas, so why don't we (you and the salesperson) just keep discussing the deal. This tactic has been used a lot and is successful many times, as during the "waiting for the keys" time a deal is made, in the dealer's favor. (Always bring a second set of keys so you can leave when you want to and return later to get the first set of keys.) A few minutes later, the service manager calls. The manager has found a hidden defect and the trade-in is worth less than the first estimate. The first estimate was $9,000. Now the true value is $7,267. Then the salesperson will say, "If the deal is bigger, the boss will let me give a little more for the trade-in." Next the salesperson makes the new car purchase bigger by adding options. If enough options are added, the value of the trade-in goes back to $9,000. The seller wins because each added option makes a lot of extra profit for the seller.

"I'll Stay at My Mistake"

The seller will make a math error on a small piece of paper when adding the price of the car and options. For example:

New car cost minus trade-in	$10,900
Plus CD player	$300
Plus special paint	$100
Plus P/T rear end	$400
Plus special seat	$200
Total	$11,600

The true total is $11,900. Most buyers do not point out the mistake. Dealers tell me 70 percent of the buyers do not point out the mistake. They just keep the "extra" money. The true new car cost minus trade-in should only be $10,600, not $10,900. The salesperson over priced the car by $300 when he agreed to $10,900. This set up the tactic of I'll stay at my mistake. The owner's objective is $10,600 for the deal. This is what the owner wants, so the owner is happy with the final deal. The salesperson is happy with the deal because a sale was made. Buyers are happy because they think they "saved" money. But they really paid $300 more than necessary. The 30 percent of the people who pointed out the "mistake" and agreed to pay $11,900 ("Everyone makes math errors once in a while") actually paid $300 more than they should have paid. This $300 is either extra commission for the salesperson and/or profit for the owner.

Unhorse the Buyer

Buyers will tell the salesperson that they will buy from this dealership or from another dealership in another town. The salesperson says, "Our car sells itself. Take our car to the other dealership. As you drive it, the car will sell itself." Buyers like this because they can test-drive the car for many miles.

But the seller has accomplished two important objectives. First, when buyers are negotiating at the other dealership, they cannot negotiate to trade in their old car. They do not have their "horse." Buyers cannot make a deal. Second, buyers must return the new car, so the seller has another chance to sell the new car. The buyer may not want to drive all the way back to the second dealer, so the buyer may just buy from the first dealership, especially if this dealer's price beats the price in the other town. And the difference doesn't have to be much, maybe only $50.

Puppy Dog

This tactic is based upon the fact that if you leave a puppy in a home with a seven-year-old child, the child and the puppy will fall in love and the puppy will stay in the home forever. In the auto sales situation, the seller will let the buyer take a new car home over the weekend. On Sunday morning, all the buyer's neighbors see the new car in the buyer's driveway and tell the buyer how lucky he or she is to be able to buy a new car. Just as with the puppy, the car now has a new home.

Agent of Limited Authority

After the buyer has agreed to a deal with the salesperson, the seller will say, "I have to get the sales manager's approval." The salesperson returns and says, "The boss says you have to pay a couple of hundred dollars more. That is only $30 more per year, less than $3 per month, really only pennies per day." The buyer has already decided to purchase the car, so what's a few pennies per day? Consider—if the dealer makes an extra $200 per car using this one tactic and in the United States dealers sell about 17 million units per year, they make an extra profit of $3.4 billion.

Budget Bogy

Early on, sellers will ask buyers how much they are planning to spend per month. Sellers want to determine the budget. They ask about a price per month because this is a small number. It may be hard for buyers to think about spending $30,000 for a car. That is a lot of money. It is much easier to think of spending $727 per month. Once the budget is established, the seller will try to sell the highest profit car within the budget range.

> **Key to Success:** To Save Money, Beware of Car Sellers' Negotiation Tactics

For most people, purchasing a car is the second most important negotiation they will ever participate in, so they must plan and be aware negotiators.

TRAVEL NEGOTIATIONS

There are lots of opportunities to negotiate when it comes to travel. We can negotiate with hotels or motels, airlines (fares, seats, canceled flight payments), car rental agencies, or negotiate for personal purchases in another country, and so on.

Lodging

Until a few years ago, most hotel rates were fixed. Generally travelers could not negotiate for a better rate. This is no longer true. Even before the economic downturn in 2001 and 2002, rates and other issues were being negotiated. I've read about a case where a person was paying $99 for a room, while next door the person was paying $175 for exactly the same room. How can this situation happen? Many hotels are now following the airline model that aims at filling all seats (rooms). Once a plane leaves, the empty seats can never be sold. Same with a hotel. Once the day is over, empty rooms are a complete loss.

Hitting the Bottom Line at Your Hotel

The first rule is to always negotiate directly with a hotel. As with any business, a hotel or motel wants to sell as much (their rooms) as possible. You do not know how full the hotel is for the nights you want to stay. If business is slow, they will not turn down a customer, especially if the customer makes a reasonable offer. I've talked to managers who told me that night desk clerks have a lot of latitude to make offers late in the evening. The potential customer standing at the desk could be the last customer for the night and any reasonable offer will be accepted. This is really extra income for the hotel, even at a low rate.

When you make reservations at a hotel, you will save money if you first ask for rates and availability for the dates you want. This is a signal to the reservation person that you have options. The result: you will get more competitive rates from the hotel because they want your business. Here are two examples.

The first example comes from a friend who had to make a business trip to Cleveland. She was told to stay at a certain hotel that was half a mile from the office she would visit. She really wanted to stay at that hotel.

Most people would call to make a reservation. She called and asked, "What are your best rates and do you have rooms for March 14–17?" She was quoted $117. Her reply was, "I know that is your rack rate, but I want your best rate for those dates." The hotel clerk said, "If you are on a business trip, I could give you the corporate rate of $109." Next my friend asked for special rates (AARP, AAA, etc.). Now the price was down just under $100. Finally she said, "I'm a government employee she teaches at San Jose State University in San Jose, California, which is a state college) and I qualify as a state government employee. What is the government rate?" The clerk said, "That is $65, but you will have to show identification to get the rate." Then she made a confirmed reservation at $65 per night and saved $62 (almost 50 percent).

Remember to always go through your list of special groups (such as AAA, AARP, special union, education, military, or corporate), before confirming a reservation. Many hotels will give a 10–20 percent discount for these special groups. Some will give up to 50 percent for military and government personnel. You should join every hotel membership club, because many times members receive special rates. Are you a stockholder in the hotel? If so, ask for the owner's rate. Are you on a hardship trip (family health problems, etc.)? If so, ask for a special discount. Also ask for any current special rates open to all (discounts, specials, etc.) at this time. Finally, ask for a cash discount and take it if possible.

Key to Success: Many Hotel Discounts Are Available—Just Ask

When you confirm, you must get a reservation number and the name of the person making the reservation. This is the key to keeping a special rate. I know of several examples where the special rate was "forgotten" or "lost" when travelers checked into the hotel.

The second example concerns a neighbor in California with family in Montana. Her sister is an avid bowler and was planning to go to Reno, Nevada to bowl in a national event. Her sister and family were staying at the hotel suggested by the bowling officials. My neighbor decided to go along and called from California to make reservations at that hotel. She got a confirmed room at $85 for two nights (Wednesday and Thursday) and $97 for one night (Friday). During their stay in Reno, they found out that her sister's room was $50 per night every night. My neighbor complained but did not get a price reduction. When her sister had made her own reservation, she had checked several hotels for rates before making a reservation at the official hotel. The hotel knew that they had to negotiate to get her business. My neighbor didn't negotiate, because she wanted that specific hotel. As a result, she paid the highest rate for her room.

Key to Success: At Hotels, Ask for Rates and Availability

It will only take a few extra minutes of your time to push the reservations person to disclose all of the hotel's different rates. They will generally do this to get extra business. If sellers know that they have your business, they have no reason to negotiate. A price reduction will reduce profit. If a seller is not sure, the seller will negotiate because any profit will be extra profit. If the profit is lower than average, that is OK, because there is more total profit.

Another key is to always call the hotel on a direct number. Never use an 800 number. The people who answer these 800 numbers are at some central location, maybe thousands of miles from the hotel. The only price these people can quote is the rack rate, which is generally very high. Generally, these people do not have the authority to negotiate prices. Also, they have no special interest in any single hotel. Keep in mind that almost every discount rate will only be available from the hotel's personnel. A final point is that the people at the central location are generally paid on volume, so they will want to make the call as short as possible.

The person at the hotel has more interest in that specific hotel and really wants it to be successful. That person generally has more authority to quote lower rates or can quickly get a manager who can give these rates. Again, the person at the 800 number is miles (thousands?) away, has little (or no) authority to give lower rates, and does not feel ownership for the specific hotel you want.

This is true when making a reservation and also when canceling a reservation. In March 2004, my son and his family planned to visit us, and we had made reservations for them to stay at a local hotel. The night before, my grandson became quite ill and was in an oxygen tent at the hospital. I called to cancel their reservation. The call was transferred to a call center. The person at the center said, "It is less than twenty-four hours, so you have to pay the first night's charge." I asked about a waiver because of a medical emergency. I was told, "Rules are rules." I asked to talk to a manager and was told, "You're not going over my head," and the person hung up on me. I called the local hotel and asked for the manager in charge. He understood the situation and understood that I was a local customer who had used the hotel in the past. The reservation was cancelled without any problem.

Key to Success: Call Direct to the Hotel, Not a National 800 Number

Another friend has saved money several times when her travel plans have changed. She calls the hotel and asks for rates. She even did this once from the hotel lobby she wanted to stay at. Why? She had two choices. The first choice was to walk up to the front desk with her large suitcase and carry-on bag and ask, "Do you have any rooms for tonight?" She would be quoted the highest rate because the front desk person would know that this customer wanted to stay at the hotel and did not have any real options. Her second choice was to take the suitcase and carry it to a phone booth (in the hotel) and call the hotel. The person who answered the phone call did not have all of the facts, did not know of her problems, and was forced to be more competitive. After getting a good rate and confirmation number, my friend then went to the front desk to check in.

If you do walk up to the desk, always wait until the desk clerk is free and no other person is checking in. This will give you a chance to negotiate a special deal without being heard by many other guests, who will want the same (or better) deal. If these other people have already checked in, they will cause problems if they discover that they paid more than you did. Remember, no matter what rate is first quoted, always ask if there is a lower rate.

Finally, after the rate has been established, ask for an upgrade to a better room or a room with a better view. Examples are golf course views, ocean views, mountain views, or maybe the quiet side of the hotel. Be sure that these requests do not result in an add-on. A person's last negotiation is to ask for free access to the refrigerator (the one with the food and drinks inside) for every day of the stay. Remember that you never get more than you ask for in a negotiation.

I stayed at a hotel in Lhasa, Tibet. Rooms on the right side of the hallway opened on to a beautiful courtyard. Rooms on the left side opened on to a street that had become an outdoor toilet. The smell in these rooms was so bad that windows could not be opened even though the temperature was in the 90s. The rooms were the same price. The people that knew this and asked, always go to the better rooms.

Problems at a Hotel May Mean Cash in Your Pocket

A year after a student was in my Business Negotiations Course in the Extension Program at the University of California, Berkeley, he called and said, "I owe you free drinks, because your class saved me $300." She then gave me all the details. She and her spouse had spent a week in Hawaii on vacation. They were very active people—golf, tennis, and so on—and spent very little time in their hotel room. (This is true for most people when they travel.) The air conditioner didn't work in their room. They filled out a maintenance report form, kept a copy, and left the form for the maid. It was never fixed. This was not a major problem for them, but my student recognized this as a negotiation opportunity. When they went to check out, their bill was over $1,200. She said to the clerk, "Your rate is for a perfect room. Our room was not a perfect room. In all this heat, we had no cold air. Here is a copy of our request. I will only pay you $600." The clerk asked her to step aside, so the clerk could handle the next person in line and to wait for a manager. She said, "I'm not moving until you correct my bill." People behind her started to make nasty comments. The clerk went into the office and quickly got the hotel manager on duty. The manager said, "We have a problem." My student said, "No, you have a problem because you are trying to charge us full price for a less than perfect room." The manager replied, "No, we have a problem. The general manager is not on the property and he is the only one that can reduce your bill to $600. I only have the authority to reduce your bill by $300." My student said, "OK, I'll help you out. Make a $300 reduction to our bill, and we'll get out of your hair." In less than ten minutes, she had saved $300 and yes, I did take the free drinks.

> **Key to Success:** There Are Many Ways to Save Money
> at a Hotel, So Ask

Air Travel

Since 9/11, the airline industry has had major problems and will do many things never before considered to retain current customers or to obtain more business.

Late Planes Can Cure a Thirst

Have you ever been on an airplane that left the gate after the departure time? (Remember, the time listed on your ticket is when the plane leaves the gate, not when it is supposed to actually take off.) I have a friend who will ask the flight attendant for free drinks when the drink cart arrives at his seat if the plane leaves after departure time. (He generally flies coach, because he does not believe that first class is worth the extra money you must pay to sit up front.)

He says, "Your airline made a contract with me that you would leave at X time. The plane didn't, and I believe that you owe me free drinks because of being late." Now the flight attendant has four options:

1. Say OK and give him two free drinks.
2. Say, "No, give me the money now, or I'm leaving."
3. Say, "OK, but don't tell anyone else I did it for you."
4. Say, "I can't give it to you because my drink cart must balance." (That is, for each empty bottle there must be money.)

For options 1 and 3 he gets his free drinks. For option 4, he suggests that the flight attendant go into first class (where drinks are free and the cart does not have to balance) for his drinks. Generally he gets his free drinks. For option 2 he has to pay, but he has lost nothing by asking. In March 2004, drinks were about $5 each on major airlines, so free drinks are a nice savings.

His best example is when he received free drinks the day after his plane was late. (And he got the free drinks, just by asking.) Here are the facts. He and his wife were flying from San Francisco to Athens, going from San Francisco to Boston to Paris to Rome and then to Athens. His plane out of Boston was seven hours late. Of course they missed their flight connection to Rome and had to stay in an airport hotel for the night. (They did go into Paris and had a few hours of sightseeing in Paris, so all was not lost.)

The next day, they took the flight to Athens, with a stop in Rome. On that flight, he asked the flight attendant for two free drinks for his wife and two for himself. His reason was that the airline had completely messed up their vacation plans, and the airline must give him something. It seemed she was a new employee and wasn't sure what to do. A senior person suggested she obtain the drinks from first class, and my friends had four free drinks. On the leg from Rome to Athens, the younger flight attendant said, "I guess you want four more free drinks." My friend said yes and he got four more drinks.

Check the Internet, Then Call the Airline

Talk to a real person and use the Internet's lowest price as the base for the negotiation. You can negotiate with this person and make sure the person understands you have the option to call a competitor. Remember hotel negotiations. When a plane takes off with empty seats, those seats will never be sold. If the person doesn't offer a better deal, ask for a supervisor.

Always Negotiate When a Flight Is Cancelled

When a flight is cancelled and costs are incurred, you must ask (demand?) that these costs be reimbursed by the airline. If the delay occurs during a mealtime, you should get a voucher to buy meals. If the delay is overnight, you should get a free hotel room. The airline will say, "We don't pay for acts of God," but most of the time they will, especially for the few that ask. If the delay is just a few hours, you should get a free phone call to tell your family of the delay.

> **Key to Success:** There Are Many Items to be Negotiated With Airlines

Car Rentals

There is not a lot of room to negotiate when renting a car, since most companies now offer free miles and a GPS system. (These used to be the areas in which experienced travelers negotiated.) If these two items aren't free, ask and you should get them. Today the best area to negotiate is getting an upgrade to a better or larger car. This should always be requested at the rental counter. They may have larger cars that are not reserved and will want to make the renter happy.

Personal Purchases When Traveling

In almost every country in the world, negotiating is a way of life and is the usual way to do business. Negotiation is a major part of the culture and lifestyle. U.S. citizens are often at a distinct disadvantage when they travel, because their negotiation skills are significantly less than those of the people they deal with. Americans pay too much and they pay more than the natives.

Some Americans will say, "I have more money than they do, so I shouldn't try to get a better price." These people might even say, "Negotiations in the second or third world are not negotiations of equals, so we should not take advantage of these people. It is not ethical to negotiate. Rich people should not haggle with poor people. The price in the third world is much lower than the price for the same item in my country, so why negotiate?" The savvy negotiator must remember that negotiating is customary in most of the world. The key is just being reasonable.

For example, if the price (in U.S. dollars) on a certain souvenir is $4.10 and you offer to pay $20 (and nothing less), this will insult the seller and reinforce the concept of the Ugly American, who is very rich. On the other hand, if you say, "I'll pay a quarter and nothing more" and never change your offer, you are again an Ugly American. In this example, the reader should shoot for paying the market price for that location—possibly a final price of about $2. This is true for items with prices marked on the item and for oral quotes.

The key to negotiating in the second or third world is always to remember that locals negotiate every day at their location and know what the market price should be. You are there for one day and know nothing about what the price should be. If your final offer is too low the seller will not sell, so if the seller accepts the offer, the seller feels it is a good deal. When the seller accepts, there should be no guilt for the American buyer.

A very large book could be filled with examples of personal purchases when traveling. For this book, one will prove the point.

Buying Blankets on the Beach

This is the introduction to a paper turned in to me as a requirement in an undergraduate negotiation course.

> During the first lecture of this negotiations course, I couldn't help but be reminded of the many vacations I have spent in Mexico and the many buyer/seller negotiations I have experienced as a result. In Mexico the bargaining process is highly ritualistic. In Puerto Vallarta, for example, there are several huge warehouses (Mercados) full of vendors with reputations of great bargaining skills. As it turns out, the reputations are based in fact. In the Mercado, the process of negotiating the deal is as important as the actual purchase. This is also true of beach vendors, although on a somewhat lesser scale. Mercado vendors have a distinct advantage in the fact that the buildings can become very hot and stuffy. Buyers can become uncomfortable. The heat and crowded conditions almost always lead to a quick close. It has become my experience that this situation translates into a situation where the buyer has paid too much. On the beach however, the buyer has several advantages. First, the buyer does not have to travel from vendor to vendor [in hot conditions]; one can merely sit back and enjoy the scenery while a multitude of vendors approach. Second the vendors really compete with each other for sales. This gives a huge advantage to the buyer.

An excellent summary of these types of negotiations.

Her paper then detailed one negotiation she had been involved in a few months before my class. Her traveling companion and she planned to purchase several Mexican cotton blankets. The paper continued, saying that since they were "familiar (if not well practiced) with the Mexican bargaining ritual, and leery of the inherent conflict involved, we decided to buy blankets together." Before leaving California, they researched the price of these blankets in the San Francisco Bay area. They found a range of prices and that much of the difference was due to overhead costs and not the cost of the blankets to the individual store. Their research found that the average price was about $30 US. They then set a target price of $15 US. (They felt this would be a fair deal for them and for the vendor.)

During their first few days in Mexico, they casually inspected blanket prices and quality in retail stores. This led them to reduce their target price to $10–15 US. The next day on the beach, they started to get serious. They sat at a table facing the beach. Waiters came and went and vendors came and went. They tried not to show too much interest. Late in the day they noticed a young man "trudging across the sand with a mountain of blankets on his shoulder." This looked like an opportunity. Jose's initial price was $41. My student countered with $5. The counter to that was $38. Then my student suggested they might buy more than one. For the next several minutes negotiations continued, including Jose buying them a beer. Finally Jose packed up all the blankets. My student made a final offer of $100 for eight blankets and actually put five $20 bills on the table. The deal was made.

FAMILY NEGOTIATIONS

This category is probably the most important in the entire book. Everyone has a very strong desire to have the best family relations possible. I don't know of anyone who wants to have bad family relationships. Papers that were written for my classes include a wide range of subjects such as teenage pregnancy, divorce, children's responsibilities, where to spend holidays, whether to move or not move for a new job opportunity, arranged marriage (the female coming from another country), wedding arrangements, and so on. It is a very long list. There are three special negotiations, husband-wife, parent-child, and partner-partner, that are key to a successful family life. A couple of examples of family negotiations are detailed below.

I believe that a key to successful family negotiations is to think of the family as you would a team (sports, theater, music group, etc.). For the individual to be a winner, the team must win. It is an old adage, but very true that there is no "I" when you spell "team."

Key to Success: There Is No "I" in a Family "Team"

We know that all win-lose negotiations become lose-lose relationships. This is a key to family negotiations. If a husband and wife continue to have win-lose negotiations, their relationship (marriage) will become a lose-lose situation and divorce is the outcome. If you really love your spouse, why would you want your loved one to be a loser? Neither spouse should want to win all the time. A good objective, for both spouses, is to let the other spouse win 75 percent of the time.

If parents have win-lose negotiations with their children when the children are young (and have very little negotiation leverage), when the children become adults it will be a lose-lose relationship. The kids will get even as adults. It is OK for parents to have win-win negotiations with their children. It is OK for the kids to win. When we teach our children negotiation skills early in life, we are preparing them for a successful adult life.

Lovers Negotiate Where to Live

An excellent paper that I received started with this introduction:

> Negotiations between two lovers can be very difficult at times. This is a story of a negotiation between two lovers. It involves one partner who has received a job offer in another location and the other partner who did not want to move. Although there are other negotiations involved, this is the negotiation that took up most of the time and was the hardest to negotiate.

Three people were involved in the negotiation: my student, his wife (who he described as "a very beautiful woman who knows what she wants and usually gets it"), and a senior vice president at the bank where my student worked. My student was a very productive worker, and the bank wanted to promote him and move him from northern California to southern California. The bank rated him so highly that the bank was willing to give him a choice of various locations.

His wife did not want to move. She was still in college at San Jose State University. She knew that she could transfer to another state college and not lose very many credits (if any), but she also knew that to get the right courses might delay her graduation. Another strong factor was that his wife's parents currently lived close to them. The negotiation took several days.

My student's initial position was this:

1. This was a big promotion and a great opportunity for his career.
2. With the extra money, his wife could visit her parents several times a year.
3. Her parents could visit them several times each year and they would get to see another part of the state.
4. If he didn't take the job, they might have to move to a smaller apartment.

5. His wife had a very good friend in Southern California and she could spend a lot of time with her.
6. It would be interesting living in another part of California.

His wife's position was this:

1. My graduation will be delayed.
2. I love my parents and do not want to hurt them.
3. There are lots of jobs.

An impasse was created. Both spouses became very emotional, yelling at each other and bringing up other problems they had (such as who made the bed and which way the toilet paper rolled). My student had a long talk with the senior vice president (who was completely objective). The bank really wanted him to move. My student was ready; he really couldn't learn any more in his current job; and they wanted to move another person into his current job as a promotion for that person. The vice president said, "Let's write down all the possible options." They developed several options. As they brainstormed, more options were discovered. The last option turned out to be the best. My student would take a lateral move (with a raise) into another department at the bank for at least a year and then he could put in for the same promotion, but in northern California.

Key to Success: Consider All Options Before Making a Decision

Key to Success: Keep Emotions Out of Negotiations

There was a successful ending to this negotiation because the senior vice president looked for options and was not emotionally involved in the negotiation. The paper started off by saying, "Negotiations between two lovers can be very difficult at times." When I returned the paper, I noted that this is a very true statement.

Negotiating for Bride, Sight Unseen

A very interesting negotiation took place between an Asian male living in San Jose, California, and an older woman also living in San Jose. The woman had a niece living in their native land. The niece wanted to move to the United States but couldn't obtain approval. Her aunt decided to find a husband for the niece, who could then obtain approval, as a spouse, to move to the United States.

The man wrote the paper. The heart of the negotiation was making a list of all of the tasks that are required in a family and determining who would be responsible for each task. The list was sent to the woman for her approval. Once this was completed, the man and the aunt negotiated the amount the aunt would pay. This was a significant sum, and it took several weeks to reach agreement.

Once the papers were signed, the woman flew to the San Jose airport, where the man met her. The last line of his paper stated, "I think I will like her."

Sunday Dinner

The wife wanted to go out to a restaurant (because she was very tired) and the husband wanted a home-cooked meal (because he had been traveling for six days). Both would not move from their position. In a very short period of time, it became a high-conflict situation because neither side wanted to let the other person win. Each wanted to win so badly that neither saw the simple solution. It was up to their seven-year-old daughter to ask, "Why can't we have pizza delivered?"

Where to Spend the Holidays

The boyfriend's family had a very strong tradition of family togetherness at his parents' home for all the major holidays (Thanksgiving, Christmas Eve and Christmas Day, and New Year's Eve), and the girlfriend's family had the same tradition. Every year there was conflict plus guilt ("If you loved your parents, you would want to spend special days with your family") and every year everyone was unhappy. They tried to spend exactly the same amount of time with each family, but that didn't help. The situation was a win-lose situation for everyone.

It was suggested that the young people not go to either parent's home. Instead they went to three different beach resorts during the next year. Their parents didn't see their children and the children didn't get to see their parents. A win-lose situation became a lose-lose situation for all. For the next holiday season, a fair schedule was accepted by all.

Key to Success: The Most Important Point to Remember in All Family and Friend Negotiations Is to Look for a Win-Win Outcome

Another consideration concerns travel. For years, parents have made all the decisions concerning travel plans. The *Conde Nast Traveler* December 2003 issue carried an excellent article titled "Who's the Boss?" It suggested that children be included in all travel decisions. The result would be happier trips and happier family members. A key statement from the article is, "Travel led my parents to see me as a short adult and for me to view them not as dictators but as co-conspirators."

Finally, the most important consideration in all family negotiations is the concept, reviewed earlier, that all win-lose negotiations will become lose-lose relations. I've been asked many times to help negotiate family problems, most of the time for a serious husband-wife problem. Generally help is not asked for until the problem has become very serious. After an informal get-acquainted discussion, I ask the husband, "Do you love your wife?" If the husband says yes, then I ask the wife, "Do you love your husband?" If the wife says yes, then we proceed with discussing the problem. If either one says no, then they need to see a lawyer, because it is too late for me to help.

I then repeat the question to the husband: "Do you love your wife?" If he says yes, then I ask him, "Why do you want to make your wife a loser in life?" Generally there is no answer, just a funny look. I repeat the question to the wife: "Do you love your husband?" If she says yes, then I ask her, "Why do you want to make your husband a loser in life?" Again a funny look. I then take them through the process of negotiation and how the process is aimed at a win-win outcome. We discuss how to make their interactions help both sides win.

Key to Success: Never Make the Most Important Person in Your Life Be a Loser

Key to Success: Never Make the Other Important People in Your Life Be Losers

Almost all family situations can become win-win situations if everyone continues to make a pledge to themselves that they will never make a loved one become a loser.

OTHER NEGOTIATIONS

This section could be the longest in this book if I listed all of the examples that are in my files. I'll give a just a very few examples to demonstrate the wide variety of negotiation situations, including situations in a restaurant, with dorm-mates, roommates, buying a mattress, and buying sports equipment. Please note that in some of these examples the writer actually lost the negotiation. These examples are very powerful when I review them in class. Sometimes when a person loses a negotiation, they learn more than if they won the negotiation.

Obtaining More in a Restaurant

The restaurant business is based on service, service, service. Most people cannot identify small differences in flavor, but everyone can tell the difference between good and bad service. Most of the time, people just accept bad service and sometimes they even give a 15 percent tip. They may not return, but they miss a negotiation opportunity. Most often, if you speak to the owner or on-site supervisor, they will either discount the bill or offer free desserts. I have twenty-seven examples in my files of people getting one of the two for bad service.

Basketball Practice at 5 a.m.

One student wrote about living in a college dorm with a varsity basketball player in the room above his who practiced his dribbling skills at 5 a.m. This was a negotiation situation and the win-win result was simple. The basketball player agreed to wait until 7 a.m. if my student bought him a six-pack of beer each week.

Roommates and Responsibilities

My student was a neat person and her roommate was not. My student was not a computer person; her roommate was. So they negotiated a win-win situation by doing for each other what they were good at. This is an important lesson for all of us.

The Mattress Will Not Fit

A young man had his very first apartment and was completely on his own for the first time. He had saved some money to furnish this apartment. The first priority, of course, was the bedroom. He saw in the paper that a local furniture store had a sale on queen-size mattresses. The young man decided that he would try out some of the skills that he had recently learned in his negotiation class at San Jose State University. He went to the store. Once inside, he saw that a king-size bed was much better and decided that he wanted it. The salesperson told him that only the queen-size beds and mattress sets were on sale.

The young man started to negotiate. After several minutes (during which the salesperson did not give in) the young man remembered that if there is an impasse, ask for the boss. So the young man asked to speak to the sales manager. The salesperson was glad to set this up, as the salesperson wanted to talk to other customers and make some sales. The young man and the sales manager negotiated for 15 to 20 minutes with no agreement. So the young man asked to talk to the owner. They talked for over thirty minutes. Finally the owner, just to get rid of the young man, called in the sales manager and told him to sell a king-size set at the discount for queen-size sets. The young man had won and he could not wait until the next class to brag about his success.

The next day the delivery truck arrived. The bed frame was brought into the apartment and put together. Next the mattress. The delivery people tried every way possible, but the mattress would not fit through the door or the window. There was just no way the mattress would go into the apartment. Finally the deliverymen gave up and took everything back to the store. The young man followed. When he arrived at the store to get a queen-size bed set, he saw that the sale signs were gone. He was told by the salesperson (yes, the same one) that the sale was over and he would have to pay full price for the queen-size set. The young man started to negotiate. The salesperson did not waste any time, and a minute later the young man was in the owner's office. The young man said he was entitled to the discount since he purchased a bed set on the day of the sale and he needed a queen-size set. The owner took this great opportunity to give the young man a detailed lesson in the facts of life (i.e., a chewing-out session). The young man had to pay for the round-trip costs of the delivery truck, but the owner liked the young man's attitude and allowed a 20% discount for the queen-size set.

A Lifetime Supply of Golf Gloves

An older woman was in the process of reentering the job market and finishing her business degree. She understood that many business deals were made on golf courses and that playing golf was one of the ways that she could increase her chances of success. She took lessons and joined a golf league (appropriately called the Duffers Club). She purchased golf shoes and was fitted for a custom set of golf clubs. After her first day, she learned the hard lesson that it is best to wear a glove on your left hand (she was right-handed).

A local golf discount store had a sale. The normal cost of a good golf glove was $15.50, but they were on sale at four gloves for $58. She saw a negotiation opportunity. She asked the salesperson, "If I double the number and buy eight, can I get them for 10 percent off ($14.50 each)?" The salesperson could not make that decision, so the salesperson got the boss and the woman made the pitch again. The boss said, "If you double the double, I'll give them to you at 15 percent off." Without thinking, the woman agreed. The woman left with sixteen golf gloves and a large charge on her credit card.

In summary, the list of items that can be negotiated is unlimited. For example, in the fall of 2002 and 2003, I taught two negotiation courses (for seniors and graduate students) at San Jose State University. Each student was required to write a paper reviewing the details of an actual negotiation during the last two years in which the student had acted as the principal negotiator. These are some of the topics (some more than once):

Membership in a health club
Insurance claim for damaged goods
Raise at work
Promotion at work
Wholesale jewelry purchase
Retail jewelry purchase
New car
Used car (Thunderbird)
Bose sound system
Tickets to a baseball playoff game
Rent on an apartment
Membership in a social club
Location of a vacation trip

Son working to become Eagle Scout
Sales of Kirby vacuums
Getting out of an arranged marriage
Purchasing a silk sari
Phone services from Sprint
Jeep repair in another state
Requirements to be a boyfriend
Child visitation times
Computer purchase at Good Guys
Family tasks before marriage
Collectibles at trade show
Grade in high school class
Dining room furniture set
Installation of TV dish
Hotel room costs
Boys'/girls' night out
Movie rentals
Sofa and chairs
Parent paying for textbooks
Router table
Computer software
Exchanging rifles for pistols
Blankets on Mexican beach
Eating at home or restaurant
Whose parents to vacation with
New boat
Cosmetics
Buy house from landlord
Fence between neighbors
Roommates' share of rent
Purchase a boxing ring
Which college to attend
Study abroad
Car insurance costs
Telephone service
Kids obeying sitter
Where to go bar hopping
Wife's trip to Europe with sister when husband doesn't want to go
Transfer to new work location with same company
Time management between a boyfriend and girlfriend

Having a civil wedding, in order to live together three years before a full
  church wedding for the families
Develop a fair schedule with siblings for cleaning the family toilets
A girl negotiating with her sister for use of dolls, toys, and special privileges
Divorce agreements, including asset splits, home ownership, and visits with
  children
How to end domestic violence without going to court

This list of examples from just two classes (plus those reviewed before)
should prove to the reader that almost every situation in life is a real
negotiation situation.

Key to Success: Almost Every Life Situation Is a
Negotiation Situation

MORE HINTS FOR SUCCESS

So far in this book, I have given many hints to success and many keys
to success. Part II includes a few other hints to success that have not
been covered so far. The most important is never to sell yourself short.
Many people feel that they have little or no leverage in negotiations, so
they don't try. If the other side senses you don't like to negotiate, or you
don't think you will do well, or you are intimidated by any negotiation
situation, or negotiation is a high-stress situation for you, the other side
will take full advantage of you.

Key to Success: Never Sell Yourself Short

There are three areas to briefly review: general hints for success, hints
for buyers, and hints for sellers.

General Hints

First, use the us-against-them tactic. That is you and me against management. Position yourself as a low-level person talking to a lower-level

person and suggest that if that person can just give you X (what you need to close the deal), you have a deal. If not, you will be forced to go to the next level. That will complicate matters. To keep it simple, let us low-level people just make the deal.

Second, use the "lower than my spouse/significant other" tactic. That is, you will accept a less favorable deal than your spouse (who is not there at the time) will. For the other person there is a choice–make a deal now or make a less favorable deal later.

Third, use the "look what you did to me" tactic. When you do business with another person or company over a period of time, there may be opportunities to use this tactic. If you didn't do well in the last (big or little) negotiation, your position must be, "Since you won the last negotiation, to be fair you must let me win this present negotiation." This is a win-win position.

Finally, use the "if" tactic. Say to your opponent, "If I do this for you, do we have a deal?" This way you get your opponent to make a commitment without making a commitment yourself. Remember, you said *if*, not that you *would* take the action.

There are also two important don'ts to remember. One, don't back the other side into a corner with no way out. Two, don't use absolute words such as *always, never,* and so on.

Finally, remember to keep emotions out of your day-to-day negotiations. When you lose control of yourself, you lose control of the negotiation.

Hints for Buyers

First, buyers must learn to use the following statements:

- Is this your best price?
- Do you give discounts to special groups?
- I'm certainly not a buyer at that price.
- For you to make a sale, you need to help me.
- Let's discuss how we can make it more affordable for me.
- I have a right to negotiate; please honor that right.
- I would love to do business with you, but you need to make these changes in your offer.
- I'm worth your best deal.
- My budget is X. That's what I can spend if you want a sale.

- This is a competitive situation; I don't have to buy from you.
- I'm part of X organization and plan to tell all the group members how you treated me (good or bad).

A second key for buyers is that time is money for salespersons. The only resource they have is their time. They have to maximize their time to make the greatest number of sales. So buyers, go slow. The more time a salesperson spends with you (and not another potential customer), the greater is the desire (the need) to make a sale to you.

Hints for Sellers

These statements are important:

- Do you want to sacrifice quality for a slightly lower price?
- Can I use you as a reference?
- If you plan to use this for a long time, consider the cost per year, not the sales price.
- Consider total cost, sales price plus maintenance, before you buy.

For both buyers and sellers, future business is always a key to success. Very seldom in buy-sell situations will the current negotiation be the last potential negotiation.

Key to Success: Future Business Is an Important Leverage Point

---

The purpose of this chapter is to show how significant negotiations can be in our personal lives. The outcome of negotiations will certainly influence our happiness and many times affect our wealth. Actually, on a percentage basis, the financial impact of personal negotiations may be greater than that of business negotiations.

The examples in this chapter are just a very small percentage of the examples I have in my files. Many of these examples come from students in my classes at San Jose State University, from my classes at the eight other universities where I've taught, from my students in in-company negotiation classes, from the public seminars I've taught, and from friends and neighbors.

Again, remember that all the principles reviewed in the first four chapters are important to having success in your day-to-day negotiations. In the twenty-first century, each person will be involved in many more negotiations than in the past.

CHAPTER 6

Telephone and Written Negotiations

Negotiations generally take place in one of three formats: face-to-face, telephone, and written. This chapter covers telephone and written negotiations.

TELEPHONE NEGOTIATIONS

There are two types of telephone negotiations: the sales pitch and the traditional negotiation where both sides have needs to be satisfied. The sales pitch "negotiation" is a one-sided high-pressure pitch to get the receiver to agree with little time to think. Almost all sales-pitch callers are working from a script and have little or no authority to make concessions and are working on commission.

For the receiver, there are three options. First, just stop the negotiation (this is a win-win solution in that neither person wastes time, if a sale is not possible). When you do, you must say a "nice no." I have a friend, Karen Clift, who always says a nice no. Generally she listens for the overview to understand the purpose of the call. Then she generally says, "Thank you very much for the opportunity, but it is not an opportunity that I want to accept at this time." The call ends on a positive note for both sides, especially for her, and she feels good about her behavior. (She can pass the Morrison Mirror Test.) Second, stretch out the call even if a sale is not possible to get revenge for being interrupted (a win-lose situation). Third, if you are interested, listen. In this option, you must listen very closely and ask lots of questions, and you must get, by mail or e-mail, a copy of the complete agreement or contract before making any purchase. Then you should get a call back the next day.

The purpose of this chapter is to offer suggestions to be more successful in a traditional negotiation.

Chester Karrass, a well-known negotiation seminar leader and author of negotiation books, wrote, "Telephone negotiations should be avoided as much as possible, since such arrangements are prone to miscommunication, therefore resulting in bad decisions."[1]

Max H. Bazerman, writing on negotiation in 2000, stated, "participants negotiating face-to-face achieve higher joint benefit, due to the higher levels of truth telling than those negotiating by telephone." He also stated, "without the presence of clear communication, participants are less likely to coordinate their moves to achieve mutual cooperation."[2]

Often telephone negotiations are harder than face-to-face negotiations, and they differ from face-to-face negotiations in several ways:

1. Generally they are much faster.
2. Due to the speed, important information may be overlooked or not covered in detail.
3. There is a lot of pressure to close the negotiation quickly.
   a. Emotions may be a key factor (e.g., anger).
   b. There may be an emergency situation.
4. There may be only one or at most a few issues.
5. The total value being negotiated is usually smaller.
6. It is harder to make calculations and listen at the same time. In face-to-face negotiations, your opponent can pause when you are writing and figuring.
7. Usually there is no agreed-upon agenda, and the agenda is set by the caller.
8. The length of the call may be a factor.
   a. Cost could be important to the side with less resources.
   b. The side that is patient has the advantage.
   c. A busy person will feel more pressure.
   d. Different time zones can cause pressure.
9. People do not address each other on a personal level as much.
   a. So you get to the point.
   b. Generally there is not enough time.
10. You have to be aware of verbal clues.
   a. Tone of voice (irritation, impatience, passion, indifference, satisfaction).

    b. Length of pauses: a pause might be a "caucus." The person is in trouble and trying to find a way out, so it is not an opening to speak.

    c. Speed of speech.

    d. Frequency of speech.

    e. Breathing methods and loudness.

11. There are no nonverbal communications.

    a. Therefore it is much easier to lie.

    b. Therefore you must do more testing of assumptions.

    c. Therefore you don't have to control physical emotional reactions, since they can't be seen.

    d. Could reduce conflict, since negative nonverbal communications cannot be seen.

    e. Harder to determine the impact of your statements.

    f. It is easier to stall.

12. Your opponent cannot look at your notes or information.

13. The caller has the advantage of surprise.

    a. If you are called, your planning time may be zero.

    b. If you are called, you usually are thinking about something else at the time of the call.

    c. If you are called, you may have a time constraint.

14. Cell phone calls can be a problem because it is easy to be distracted, especially when driving.

15. If you call, your planning time must be adequate.

16. Silence can convey powerful messages.

17. Interruptions may affect the negotiation.

18. You must pay more attention to the exact words.

    a. Very important to take detailed notes.

    b. Very important to review and reconfirm many times.

    c. Always get names and titles before serious discussions.

19. For some people it is much easier to negotiate, since they don't have to look the other person in the eye (the shy person has a better chance).

20. For others it is harder, since they cannot intimidate their opponent.

21. Generally, these are one-on-one negotiations, especially personal negotiations.

    a. Should be easier for strong negotiators.

    b. Should be harder for weak negotiators.

22. You will need many more recaps, since it is easier to lose track of all the items discussed and positions taken.

23. Location may be less formal (home rather than an office).

24. The person with most knowledge of the subject has a major advantage.

25. The person with most knowledge also is generally most confident.
26. Time of the call is very important.
    a. Just before lunch or the end of the day generally means it will be a short call.
    b. If negotiating from a weak position, pick a time that is very comfortable for the opponent.
27. Finally, we use our phones in many situations that are not negotiations (calls to family, friends, etc.), so many people make the mistake of not taking a phone negotiation as seriously as a face-to-face negotiation. Often they forget that this is a negotiation and not a cordial conversation.

The savvy negotiator will continue to review these differences. Most of the time when we hear the word *negotiate* we think of face-to-face negotiations. In the twenty-first century, more negotiations will take place over the phone (or by Internet). To ensure success in phone negotiations, savvy negotiators must remember and use to their advantage the differences of phone negotiations.

Finally, I should review seven major ways in which telephone negotiations are unique. First, the negotiator cannot see the other person. This is very important, because we know that when two or more people are interacting and negotiating, there are more nonverbal communication messages than verbal (oral) communication messages. It is very important to remember that it is much easier to lie with your mouth than with your body. Many studies have found that nonverbal communications are significantly more honest than verbal communications. During a phone negotiation, it is much harder to read your opponent and much easier to lie.

Second, most telephone negotiations are much shorter in duration. This is especially true for long distance calls, because there is a significant cost involved and the rate structures are weighted against business calls. They change as competition changes, but there are usually different rates for calls after 5 p.m. Many companies have special telephone services, such as in-house phone networks or special contract rates, to help them achieve a lower cost per call. Whatever the cost-reduction techniques, there is still a cost, and most people who negotiate on the phone are always aware of the cost and try to get it over with quickly. Those who negotiate from home seldom have any special quantity discount rates, and time is very important to them. In every case, people who negotiate on the phone are always aware of the cost. Even if this awareness is in the subconscious, it still will influence the call.

Third, most phone negotiations are for smaller values. Throughout the world, there is common agreement that major negotiations must be completed in person. (With fast modern jets, it is easy to be anywhere in the world in one day to negotiate.) Of course, the definition of *major* is very dependent upon the size of the organizations involved. This is a key concept. For most business negotiations, it is related to the size of both your organization and your opponent's organization. For most individual negotiations, it is related to the comparison of the value of the negotiation to the income of the individual. For a company the size of Microsoft, a $100,000 negotiation will not be considered major. But for a small start-up company negotiating with Microsoft, it may be the most important negotiation of the year. For a young high school graduate buying a first car, a $7,000 negotiation will be considered the most important in life. For a successful movie or sports star, $7,000 may be less than the average price of Christmas presents given to helpful assistants. Each negotiation has its own scale. "Major" negotiations are generally conducted in person and "minor" negotiations are generally conducted by phone.

Fourth, the planning time for a phone negotiation is usually very short and in many cases it is zero. Many times, one side simply decides that a phone call negotiation must be made and picks up the phone. The side that starts the negotiation may have time to plan and think about what will be said, at least the opening statements and first positions. Often this is a buyer (industrial or personal) who needs an item. The smart buyer will use a short planning period. Unfortunately, sometimes the person will just pick up the phone and start dialing. Whatever the case, there is not a lot of time to complete a scientific planning process such as the process outlined in *The Prenegotiation Planning Book*. The receiver of the call generally is not aware of the need or the fact that this call is about to be made, and cannot do any planning. In many business situations, this is the seller's side of the negotiation. Some people suggest that if you are surprised by a business phone negotiation, you should hang up and not call back until you have prepared for the negotiation. This may be very hard if you are the seller. For many personal negotiations, it is the potential buyer who is surprised (especially at dinnertime) and has no planning time.

Fifth, many phone negotiations are based upon an urgent need, rather than a long-range need. For example, a factory may have run out of a certain part and need replacements now to keep production going. The plant manager goes to purchasing and says, "Call ABC Company right now and get the status of our open purchase order. Have the material delivered as soon as possible." A personal example could be a washer that has broken down and needs to be fixed today.

Sixth, many phone negotiations are based upon the need to deliver a message. This is generally a negative message because the individual does not want a face-to-face confrontation. In the business world, this could be a boss who calls a subordinate to tell him his performance is not meeting objectives and he is in trouble. In the personal world, it could be a person breaking off a long-term relationship. In general, when we give good news to another person, we want to give it in person. We can share the news with the person and feel good about it, and the meeting is very positive. In general, most people do not like to give bad news in person, so they use the phone to give it.

Seventh, in a large majority of phone negotiations, when the negotiation is completed, the two sides have a different opinion of the agreement. All phone negotiations must be confirmed in writing ASAP. Since the purpose of the negotiation is to set the ground rules for a future relationship, the two sides must agree on the exact content of the agreement.

Key to Success: Always Confirm Phone Negotiations in Writing

For several years in my Negotiation and Conflict Resolution courses at San Jose State (MBA and senior level), the students have completed a phone negotiation. It is a simple management-labor negotiation for a new contract. The negotiation is held during a regular class period (there is no regular class that day) and is limited to two hours. It is a one-on-one negotiation. The students exchange numbers and most negotiate from home. After the negotiation, each person writes down the agreement. They are told not to discuss the agreement after the end of the negotiation. They seal their copy of the agreement and turn it in at the next class.

The students assume they will be graded (grades are 0–100 with no curve) on how well they represented their principal in the negotiation. They really negotiate as hard as possible. Generally there is a lot of conflict during the negotiation. The actual basis for the grade is how well the two written agreements match. If the two contracts are exactly the same, both students get grades of 100. For each difference (for example, labor says "two more vacation days" and management says "one more vacation day"), I subtract 5 points. The average grade is 55, meaning there are nine differences between the contracts. The learning objective is that we must always confirm phone negotiations. The best time to confirm is before the call is completed. You should completely review all the contract terms and get your opponent to confirm the agreement. Then agree that the contract will be firm after both sides have reviewed the written confirmation of the contract (by e-mail).

Another case study is completed by e-mail. This is for the remodeling of a kitchen. The students have a week to negotiate. After reaching agreement, each student e-mails me his or her copy of the agreement. The grading system is the same, and because everything is written, the average grade is 90.

These are the seven major ways that phone negotiations are unique. You could add other factors from your personal life that show how unique phone negotiations are and how important they have been to you. To be successful in phone negotiations, the savvy negotiator must have all of the skills necessary to negotiate in normal situations, plus special skills for phone negotiations.

A basic understanding of the process of negotiation is a must to improve your telephone negotiation skills. Several books have been written, in great detail, on this subject, and I encourage each reader to develop a personal negotiation library. To improve your future phone negotiations, here are three important considerations:

1. A review of the differences in the rituals of face-to-face negotiations and those of phone negotiations
2. A review of the major negotiation tactics used in phone negotiations
3. A checklist to be used during phone negotiations

Rituals

Differences and Similarities to Face-to-Face Negotiations

Most face-to-face negotiations follow a structured ten-step ritual:

1. Introductions
2. Background music (talk about weather, sports, etc.)

3. Why we are here today
4. History of the relationship
5. Issue definition (what do we disagree on)
6. Conflict
7. Compromise
8. Frame the solution (outline the areas of agreement)
9. Agreement or Agreement in principle (An agreement in principle negotiation is one in which one (or both) side(s) of the negotiation table do not have full authority. For example, in union negotiations the union negotiator must get the members approval before it is a firm contract.)
10. Help your opponent justify the deal to the opponent's boss

Following this ritual is a key to success in face-to-face negotiations. Too many amateur negotiators try to move too quickly and lose. This is especially true in international negotiations. The savvy negotiator understands that we just cannot rush any negotiation. Remember, the patient negotiator generally does best.

Most phone negotiations have only five steps:

1. Introductions
2. Issue definition
3. Conflict
4. Compromise
5. Agreement

There is a final step in phone negotiations when a written document is exchanged to confirm the agreement.

The Steps in Phone Negotiations

1. *Introductions.* Be sure to write down the name and title of the persons you are talking to before discussing the reason for the phone call. Also try to determine the power and authority this person has in the negotiation. Once I was in a negotiation with representatives of the People's Republic of China. I exchanged business cards with the lead negotiator. His title was deputy director of a district in China. My first impression was that this person had a lot of power. During one of the breaks, one of my team members was talking to a person on the other

side and found out that the lead negotiator was only a maintenance supervisor for a seven-block area in Beijing. The lead negotiator had no power and was just trying to get as much information and as many concessions from us as possible without giving anything away. Later the real power would enter into the negotiation.

> **Key to Success:** Always Know Who You Are Negotiating With

2. *Issue definition*. Again, you must write down the issues to be discussed. After you have written them down, repeat them to the other person to ensure that there is at least agreement on what the issues are.

3. *Conflict*. Remember, one reason we negotiate is because there is conflict, and to be successful you must be comfortable with conflict.

4. *Compromise*. Be sure to give and get, not just give. Take lots of notes and write down as much as possible. At each stage of the negotiation, be sure to recap. Do not let the other side try to confuse you.

5. *Agreement or nonagreement*. Again, remember to get the final agreement in writing and be sure that if the written agreement is not what you believed it was, you can terminate the contract without penalty.

Tactics

One of the most important tactics that are used in most phone negotiations is the deadline. That is, one side tells the other side that we must act before X date. There are many "reasons" such as these:

There will be a price increase.
We will run out of stock.
Sale ends on . . .
Labor contract expires on . . .
Production starts on . . .

The important point to remember is that a deadline is only a real deadline if both sides accept that date. Many times in my life I've purchased items at the sale price long after the sale was over, just by asking. Many times I've been able to get the old price weeks after a price increase.

Mystical third party is another very important tactic the savvy negotiator will understand. The mystical third party is anyone or anything that is not part of the negotiation that is used as the reason for a negotiator's position. Examples of mystical third parties are:

Company policy
Budget will not allow
My boss said . . .
The customer wants . . .
The computer cannot do that

A very good example of this tactic is when the negotiator says, "It is against our company policy to pay the freight costs, so that will be added to your bill." How can you argue with company policy? Especially in a short phone negotiation. It could be possible to talk to the executive in charge of company policies to ask for a change, if the person would ever talk to you, but in 99.9 percent of negotiations you just don't have the time. Another example that is used a lot is, "My customer wants to reduce our price by 10 percent, so all of our suppliers must reduce their price to us by 10 percent to keep our business." It would be very hard to talk to the customer to verify this statement.

A classic example happen to me during a negotiation with a software company in the Silicon Valley. I was negotiating to teach several in-company negotiation workshops. My terms for invoice payment are net in ten days. The other person said, "I would like to agree to pay you in ten days, but our computer is programmed to only write checks once a month, so you will have to wait for payment." This was from a person who knew all about computers and how to program them.

Another important tactic is *comparative options*. One side gives the other a choice between two options: do you want to do it this way or that way? This lets the other side make a decision. For example, a spouse could say, "Dear, do you want to go to a movie this weekend or do you want to go and see my mother?" The other spouse does not want to see the mother-in-law and quickly says, "Let's go to a movie." The second spouse made a decision and the first spouse did what he or she wanted to do. During a rapidly moving phone negotiation, people can take advantage of the other side and obtain what they want in the negotiation very easily by using this tactic. Remember, there are always other options. In the above example, the second spouse could say, "Why don't we play golf together this weekend?" This introduces a third option.

Two tactics, *always use an authority for your position* and *all numbers must be precise to the third decimal point*, are used together many times.

In negotiations, we are careful when it comes to trusting what the other side says, because we know we are in a negotiation. But we tend to believe and trust what authorities say. Good negotiators will always use an authority to justify their position.

Examples:

The design engineer said . . .
The Bible said . . . (for a Sunday sermon)
Professors at Yale said . . .
Research results are . . .
The *Operations Management Journal* had an article that said . . .
The *Financial Times* stated . . .
The Federal Reserve reported that . . .

For a number to be believable, the number has to sound realistic. If I'm asked to give an estimate of how long it will take to wind eleven transformers and say "22 hours," you will think that is just an estimate (2×11). If I say, "It will take 22.35 hours," you will think that is an exact number. You will believe that I had exact facts as a base to determine my answer.

Here is an example of how these two tactics are often used together. A purchasing manager is talking to a supplier. Which statement is more believable?

A. "Your quality record shows a rejection rate of 6 percent and that is too high."
B. "During my preparation for this negotiation, I talked with our quality assurance manager (use authority), and the manager told me that during the last fourteen months your rejection rate has been 6.272 percent [exact number] and that is too high."

We all would agree that statement B is much more believable than statement A.

Snow with facts is another popular tactic. That is, on the phone, one side gives lots of facts and numbers in order to confuse the other side. That side's position is, since I have all the facts I must be right on everything. This works especially well with right-brain people who are not very good with math. You must slow down the other person. Ask that person to repeat the facts so that you can write them down.

The *quickie* tactic is used to get you to agree on an issue that has not been discussed by coupling it with a second issue. For example, a buyer and seller have agreed that the cash terms for this contract will be a 1 percent discount if paid in ten days and net if paid in thirty days. The seller then tries to use a quickie to get a free on board (FOB) point by saying, "OK, then we have agreed that the terms will be 1 percent in ten days and net in thirty days and it will be FOB my factory, which is the industry standard." The seller hopes the buyer will agree and give the seller the FOB point the seller wants. You cannot use this tactic for major issues. It can be very successful for small issues.

Many phone negotiators will use *yes, but* frequently. You will argue with their position and try to negotiate with them. When you have finished, they will say, "You are right and I agree completely with your position of X, but we can't do that for you." You are lulled to sleep when the other side is agreeing with you and sometimes you fall for their position. In these cases, *but* is a big eraser in that it erases all the words used before the *but*.

An *appeal to emotion* is very successful with caring people. A negotiator may state that he must have one more sale today to meet his quota for the month. If the quota is not met, the negotiator will not receive his bonus and he will not be able to do something for his family (for example, pay his daughter's college tuition).

Big-big-little is used a lot by children. Using this tactic, the negotiator asks for something big that the negotiator knows you will turn down. Then the negotiator asks for something else big that you are certain to turn down. Then the negotiator asks for something the negotiator really wants and lays guilt on you, saying, "Aren't you ever going to say yes?" This is a good family example:

SON: Dad, can I use the big family car this Friday night starting at 4 p.m.? I want to hang out with the guys for a while, then have dinner, then go to the football game, then out to a couple of parties and then have breakfast with my friends. I should be home before 11 Saturday morning.

DAD: No way.

SON: Well, then could I have it at 7 p.m. to go to the game, the parties, and breakfast?

DAD: No way.

SON: Don't you ever say yes to me? Can't I have the car to go to the game and a couple of parties and be home early?

The dad is in a real bind and will generally say OK.

In a tactic called *doomsday*, the other person will tell you all of the bad things that will happen to you if you don't make an agreement right now. For example, "If you don't order today, the items will not be shipped in time to arrive before Christmas Day. Do you want your family to be disappointed on Christmas Day?" "If you don't have your tuition check to give to us today, you will not be allowed to register for this semester and will not graduate on time. Think of all the salary you will miss starting on a job at least six months late."

Beware of the *stretch-out* tactic. This tactic is used to get an order where delivery is critical. The supplier gets the order by stating that they will deliver on time. They know that they can't deliver on time but say they can just to get the order. They hope that something will happen (an electrical outage, a snowstorm, etc.) that they can blame their lateness on. When the savvy negotiator suspects that this tactic is being used by the opponent, the savvy negotiator will propose a penalty clause. Here is an example of how to do this:

BUYER: Are you sure that you can deliver on time?

SUPPLIER: Yes, no problem.

BUYER: Are you sure that you have talked to all of your key people, especially in the production department, and they have agreed to ship on time?

SUPPLIER: As I said, we will have no problem shipping on time.

BUYER: Then it should not be a problem for you to accept a penalty clause in our contract. This will cost you nothing since you will ship on time and will not be late.

The last tactic to review is familiar to most of us—*bait and switch*. The seller talks to you about this item that is on sale, but after a short discussion shifts to another item that "will do a much better job of satisfying your needs." Of course, this second item has a much higher price.

Phone Negotiation Checklist

Point 1: Who Negotiates on the Phone

Situations and conditions. Some of the major situations are: expediting materials or supplies that are on order, negotiating to place a purchase order, getting important information, selling a product or service, and the high-pressure sales pitch.

How often? Many people in business negotiate daily on the phone. For others it is not very often (except for the high-pressure call).

Why must we negotiate? If we make the call, it is because we need something. If we receive the call, it is because we have something that the other person wants (a sale, material shipped, etc.).

What are the advantages and disadvantages? The major disadvantage is that we cannot see the other person. We can't read nonverbal communications. Another disadvantage is that the negotiation generally goes too fast. An advantage is that phone negotiations are cheap. There are no expenses for airfare, hotel meals, and so forth. Also, phone negotiations don't take a lot of time.

Beware of speakerphones. Refuse to let the other side use a speakerphone. There may be people in the room that should not be there or that will give aid to the person speaking.

Point 2: The Difference in Who Makes the Call

First to speak to outline reason for call. This is an absolute must. To be most successful, the person making the call must make a meaningful statement outlining the purpose of the call.

Needs assessment as to who has the greatest need. As with all negotiations, the side with the greatest need will have more pressure to get a quick settlement. In face-to-face negotiations, we can read this pressure from nonverbal communications. For telephone negotiations it is harder. A general condition is that the caller has the greatest need. So callers must do two things. First, they must try to mask the urgency of their need, and second, they must work at showing the receiver that a need of the receiver can also be satisified.

Getting attention and creating interest. The first few seconds of a telephone negotiation are critical. The caller must be able to show the receiver that there is something for the receiver if the call continues. The receiver must believe the caller can satisfy a need. Does the telephone call have something to deliver or satisfy a need?

It's OK to call back. The person who sets the time of a future call has control.

Time considerations. Since phone negotiations are usually much shorter than face-to-face, we generally get to the point much faster. Time is always a factor. If you are calling to get something from the other side, it is best to see you are calling at a good time. If not, get a call-back time. You will have a much better chance of winning if the other side is not under time pressure.

Recently, a perfect example happened to me. I went to my branch office of the Wells Fargo bank. I wanted to complete simple transaction, moving money from an IRA to checking (a must since I was seventy in March 2005). The person I talked to said he could do that and then started a high-pressure sales pitch for me to buy some "special" annuity that "would be just right for me." I kept trying to bring the person back to my need, but the person refused and kept selling. I wasted an hour of my time on a task that should have taken ten minutes at most. A few weeks after that I invested some funds—not with Wells Fargo. Had the person taken care of my needs, he would have later made a nice commission.

When to lengthen for your benefit. If you sense a high level of urgency to get an agreement quickly, you will always stall. The more time the person spends with you, the more desire there is to get an agreement (time is money), and you may get a better offer to get the deal completed.

Point 3: Basic Distractions

Situations not normally found in face-to-face negotiations. On the phone, as I said previously, it is much easier to lie for an advantage. For example, in a business negotiation a person might say, "Hold on for a minute. My boss just walked in," as a way of getting time to think out a problem. A good response to test this statement might be to ask to say hello to the boss.

Distractions you cannot control. This includes anything that happens on the other end of the line. Many times, people will use a distraction to put pressure on you (especially if there is a time constraint). You must be patient. Don't let the other side get to you.

Distractions you can control

- Put out a "do not disturb" sign if at work.
- Turn off pagers, cell phones, and so on.
- Unless you are taking notes, put your computer to sleep.
- If you are at home, turn off TV, radio, and so on.
- Tell the kids to play by themselves.
- Don't doodle.

Point 4: Nonverbal Clues

A major problem with phone negotiations is that you cannot see opponents and read their nonverbal communications, especially their body language. There are a few clues that you should be aware of.

Tone of voice. Most of the time, when the tone of voice changes, it means the other side is under pressure. This is true if the tone goes up or down.

Speed of speech. Most of the time, when speech speeds up, it means one of several things, such as:

- The person is under pressure.
- The person is not telling the truth.
- It is a one-sided deal in the other person's favor.
- It is a very hard-sell situation.

When the speed slows down, it means the other person is thinking about what to say and exactly how to say it. Refer to the section in chapter 3 concerning half-truths. Be aware that many statements given when speech is slowed down could be well-thought-out half-truths.

If you believe a statement to be a half-truth, there is a way to check this out. Generally, we ask people to repeat their statement. They will say exactly the same words. I strongly suggest you ask people to *restate* their statement. This will cause them to use different words that may disclose the half-truth.

> **Key to Success:** Ask Opponents to Restate Their Statements, Not Repeat

Throat clearing. Means the person is not sure what to say (unless the person really has a cold). Two other reasons: something was said that surprised the person, or the person is not telling the truth.

Sighs and heavy breathing. There is a lot of power in saying "Hmmm." This may seem like complete acceptance of your statement, but generally it does not signal acceptance. This is very important if you are negotiating with a person from the far east. Many times that person will say "yes" to your statement. They mean "I understand what you said." They do not mean "I accept your proposal."

> **Key to Success:** "Hmmm" Is Not Acceptance

Silence. If you hear silence, something has come up in the negotiation that the other side was not prepared for and they need time to think up an answer. This is really a caucus. It is best to let them think, because a new or better deal might be proposed.

Point 5: Alternatives in an Impasse

You have four options when there is an impasse in phone negotiations. First, you can hang up. Second, you can make a new proposal. Third, you can try humor. Fourth, you can just give in.

Significant dangers if you hang up. Unless it is a high-pressure sales call, hanging up can be very dangerous. In face-to-face negotiations, if you start to walk out, the other side can stop you and continue the negotiation. They can use humor or a new proposal to get you back to the table. Also, you can read their nonverbal communications to understand that they really want to continue the negotiation. With a hang up that is impossible. A hang up may mean that whatever the opportunity was, it is now lost forever.

When you must hang up and why. If you feel that any agreement will be one-sided, it is not in your best interests to continue.

How to communicate that you are ready to hang up. It is very important that you give a clear message to the other side that you are ready to hang up. This must be as clear as possible and repeated.

Making a new proposal is not as difficult as it seems. The best way to make a new proposal is to use the word *if* (see chapter 3). When you use *if*, you are not making any commitment to the other side. Remember the example of a seller who says, "If we agree to pay the freight, will you give me an order?" Should the buyer say yes, the buyer has made a commitment, but the seller has not. Besides being a good questioning technique, this is a powerful way to break an impasse. You have no obligation, but you have restarted the negotiation. This is a good way of trying to save face for the other side while at the same time saving your own face.

Humor can be powerful. A friend has a windup toy that he takes with him to all negotiations. If there is a serious impasse, he takes out the toy, winds it up, and puts it on the table. The toy goes in circles. Then he says, "I feel that we are going around in circles just like that toy. Do you agree?" The other side usually laughs and says, "Yes!" They now have agreed on something and they can restart the negotiation.

Final thought. *Never negotiate on the phone while driving a car.* Negotiating is a full-time job for the savvy negotiator. To be successful, the negotiator must listen intently at all times and think about what to say next. There is absolutely neither time nor attention for a person to safely drive a car.

Key to Success: Never Negotiate While Driving

WRITTEN NEGOTIATIONS

The best way to visualize the difference between written and phone negotiations is this example. In high school I met Fred Judson, who became my best friend for life. We played a lot of chess (he still teaches chess). For most of our matches, we used a time clock. He attended the University of Connecticut and I went to Trinity College in Hartford, Connecticut. While at college, we played chess by postcard. Phone negotiations are like chess using a timer. Written negotiations are like chess by postcard.

Many of the recommendations about telephone negotiations also apply to written negotiations, so you should review the previous material. There are a few differences:

1. Written negotiations take more time.
2. You can think ahead in written negotiations.
3. It is much harder to use tactics (especially sneaky tactics).
4. It is much easier to always focus on the total package, not just each issue.
5. Power is more balanced, because of the time delay.
6. Fast thinkers lose their advantage.
7. It is much harder to intimidate the other side.

One very big danger of written negotiations is that the negotiation will become a zero-sum negotiation.

E-Mail Negotiations

Today the most commonly used form of written negotiations is e-mail. There are several pros and cons that savvy negotiators must be aware of when they use e-mail. The purpose of this section is first to review a few examples of e-mail negotiations to get a feel for the current state of the art. Then there is a discussion of the advantages and disadvantages of using e-mail in the negotiation process. Finally, I share a couple of hints to maximize your results when negotiating via e-mail.

Recently, a very good friend purchased a new home using e-mail. He was in Idaho and was moving to Texas. After a fact-finding trip to Texas that identified a couple of good prospects, my friend had to return home to finish his responsibilities at his old job. My friend gave the agent in

Texas authority to make an offer (the offers were different, but within my friend's budget) on both houses at a number that was very low, but still in the ballpark. My friend was at work but had his personal computer there. The agent then met with the owners, and their agent, of the top-priority home. The agent had her wireless computer and e-mailed the counteroffer. The agent also included confidential information and negotiating ideas. The negotiation, with a couple of offers and counteroffers, lasted about an hour. The two sides were close, but could not agree on a final number.

The agent then went to the second-priority home and started negotiating with the owner and her agent. During that negotiation, the agent received an e-mail from the agent for the first home. This e-mail stated that the owners had reconsidered and would accept the last offer from my friend. At the second house, the agent asked for a ten-minute break and e-mailed my friend. My friend and his agent had an in-depth online discussion and decided to purchase the first-priority house. The agent made a graceful exit from the second house and by e-mail officially accepted the offer on the first home. Only because of real-time information did my friend get the house that he really wanted.

This is a good example of the positive use of e-mail in the negotiation process. The secret is that there were human inputs and evaluations in the process. The negotiation was not exclusively by e-mail, but it was facilitated by the medium.

A second example is the contract for this book. I had a number of discussions and negotiations with my editor, Nick Philipson, at Praeger concerning the details of this book project. Within a few hours, I would receive an e-mail from him confirming the substance of a phone discussion. Since this was in writing, it was official and there was no doubt about the exact agreement. If there were any problems, a follow-up phone call would clarify the details. An e-mail would confirm the second call. Our negotiations were very successful, and this book is in print. I believe this is a win-win-win. A win for me, as the book was published. A win for Nick, as his company will make a nice profit. A win for you, as your future negotiations will be more successful. Also, with these e-mails Nick and I have a complete history of all our discussions.

I feel that this is the best use of e-mail in the negotiation process—that is, to formalize discussions on the phone or in person. When we negotiate orally, there can be differences of opinion about what was said.

(Remember the example in this chapter about phone negotiations in my university negotiation courses.) Using an e-mail to follow up saves a lot of trouble now and especially down the road. (Remember the discussion of perceptions versus reality.)

My very good friend Karen Clift collects salt-and-pepper shaker sets. I knew nothing about this hobby before I met her and have learned a lot in the last year. There is a major national organization dedicated to this hobby that has a newsletter, sales exchange, and even a national convention. We have gone to auctions where many very different items were offered to bid on sets or a large tray full of sets of shakers. The auction house has digital pictures of each lot to be auctioned and puts this data online a couple of weeks before the auction date. This allows people who can't be in the auction house to bid by e-mail on the items they want.

There is a major problem with using e-mail in this way that the savvy negotiator must be aware of. I have never seen a situation in which the e-mail bid was just a small amount above the last oral bid and became the winning bid. The auctioneer at the start of the bidding process would announce, "I have an e-mail bid," before she opened the bidding. (She did not disclose the amount of the bid.) A very large percentage of the time, after a few bids she would say, "The e-mail bid is out." When the e-mail bid was the winner, it was generally at least 25 percent above the last bid.

Using e-mail in this situation is very risky in that the e-mail bid is generally either much too low or much too high. It is better to find a person or agent to be at the auction and use a cell phone to keep you in the live bidding process.

Another friend has a small transformer business. He was asked to bid by a potential new customer for a 100-piece lot of a new design, with the expectation that the winner would get more business down the road. He knew very little about the customer and didn't have time for a long investigation.

He bid by e-mail (with the notification mode on, so he knew the bid was received). Everything was spelled out in great detail. My friend didn't leave any room for future movement. Within a couple of hours, my friend was notified that he won the order. Later in discussions with an engineer, my friend learned that his bid was 17 percent low. He had left significant money on the table. Had my friend been able to talk to these people and negotiate orally, he could have made a lot more profit.

This is an example of what can happen with a fast one-way e-mail response. Since it is all in writing, it cannot be taken back. Since you cannot read nonverbal communications, you have no idea about the quality of your bid. Since there is no give and take, you cannot modify your offer (up or down).

Advantages of E-mail Negotiations

There are nine distinct advantages of using e-mail in the negotiation process. They are not listed by priority. Each advantage, when used correctly, can help the savvy negotiator to be successful in the future.

1. Today almost everyone is computer savvy and many have used computers all their lives. These people are more comfortable using computers than using old-fashioned "snail" mail. Many people spend hours each day in front of the computer screen. When your opponent in a negotiation is comfortable, you have a better opportunity for creating a win-win situation.
2. E-mail is less formal than snail mail. This is an advantage, especially with younger people who have grown up in a significantly less formal atmosphere.
3. E-mail is much faster than any other written form of negotiation. The U.S. Postal Service has much better service than most people think. Still, it takes a day or two to send and receive a letter in the United States. Private delivery services (UPS, FedEx, etc.) can guarantee overnight delivery. This is still a wait of twelve hours or more. This delay is especially true with international negotiations. Recently we were on photo safari in southern Africa. The postcards that we sent took about two weeks to get to the United States.
4. E-mail can record and confirm oral negotiations. After a discussion on the phone or in person, an e-mail will put all of the agreements in writing. This way both sides can take their time and review the information to be sure it is what they agreed to during the negotiation. This will completely confirm the oral negotiations. If you missed something that your opponent said, you will find it in the written word. If there is a problem with exact commitments, timetables, and so on, it will be easy to see in the written e-mail.
5. E-mails are very timely and can be real-time communications. The house-buying example demonstrated this advantage. Time is money. This is the mantra for the twenty-first century. Real-time e-mails save a whole lot of time.

6. E-mails are very timely and fast. Yet at the same time, since they have to be typed, there is time for you to compose your thoughts and write exactly what you mean. The ability to be very precise is a great advantage. You should never miss what you want to say or confirm because you have the time while typing to think about the completed negotiation. During oral negotiations, many times we are not as exact or precise as we must be to have a good contract. Oral discussions can be vague or approximate in nature. Once it is put in writing, information must be very exact.

7. As long as both sides understand, e-mails are very good for presenting initial positions. They are especially great for identifying areas that are in conflict between the two sides that must be negotiated. Be careful to ensure that your opponent doesn't believe that your position is "take it or leave it."

8. E-mail is good when used to ask for information. This reduces time in negotiations. It is an efficient way of asking questions and getting answers.

9. E-mails are good when they ask for an action. This is a one-way communication and both sides understand the purpose of the request.

To summarize, using e-mail has several advantages in your future negotiations. Please remember that it is my firm belief that the very best use of e-mail in negotiations is to confirm oral negotiations, whether they are on the telephone or face-to-face.

Disadvantages of E-mail Negotiations

The savvy negotiator must understand these major disadvantages (not by priority):

1. Once something is in writing, it cannot be taken back. Yes, there is case law that says an obvious error cannot be enforced, but this doesn't cover a poor offer or a stupid position on any issue in the negotiation.

For example, if a company quoted $10,000 instead of $100, the company could get out of the quote. But if it quoted $10,000 instead of $8,000, it would be held to the bid.

A lawyer friend once told me that often during a trial she will not object to a question or answer that is not legal because she doesn't want the jury to remember the question or answer. She said, "I hope that the jury will forget it and my client will be better off. An objection will highlight that question. Once I object, I cannot take it back."

2. The e-mail system is not completely safe. Any average hacker could get into your system and read all your e-mails. The competition would then know your offer and could act to better that offer.
3. Even when you delete data, they can stay somewhere in the computer.

Here's an example. I live in Palo Alto, California, and San Carlos is a town between Palo Alto and San Francisco. A woman in San Carlos purchased a used computer. When she hooked it up and started using it, she found a lot of data from the original owner, including his Social Security number, bank account numbers, passwords, and so on. She was an honest person and returned the computer.

I have a friend who works with confidential and top-secret data. A few years ago, he purchased a new computer. He destroyed his old computer with a sledgehammer and then put the parts into a saltwater bath for thirty days to ensure that all the data were destroyed.

4. It can be hard to make suggestions or float ideas using e-mails. Once in writing, an idea takes on a more formal or official quality. This could hurt a negotiation position later in the process. Many successful negotiations have found a compromise solution after a "what if" statement.
5. The negotiation can quickly fall into just a bargaining process. For example, I offer $27. You offer $14. I counter with $22. Then you say $17. On and on this goes. It becomes just like buying a rug.
6. E-mails can be used to ask for information. This can be a trap, since the information can be used against you during any future negotiation.

For example, I once made a lot of money in a negotiation by finding out that my opponent had a special deal with a bank to get a very low interest rate. I asked an innocent question: "What does money cost for your company?" My opponent wanted to brag about his great negotiation with his bank to get a very low rate. Later, when I asked him to hold a lot of inventory for me, he couldn't say no because it really wouldn't cost him very much money and I knew it. The innocent question early in the negotiation had cost his company a lot later on. Many e-mails look innocent but can be bombshells later in the negotiation.

7. E-mail negotiations can easily become zero-sum negotiations in which there is a winner and a loser. It is very hard to add value using e-mails alone to negotiate.

To summarize, there are several disadvantages of using e-mail in negotiations. The most significant disadvantage is that once anything is in writing, it becomes official.

Hints for Successful Use of E-mail in Negotiations

The savvy negotiator will use all the advantages of e-mail and avoid the disadvantages. Here are three more tips for success:

1. Before you make any quote or offer by e-mail, you must find out if all bids are considered firm and whether the contract will be based on the points in the e-mail. Be sure to ask whether there will be a BAFO (best and final offer). If there is a BAFO, will it be offered to all bidders, or just the best bidders? That is, should you give your best shot now or do you have a second chance?
2. Word your offers "based on these assumptions." That allows you to retract the offer if there is something you really don't understand. If you understand everything, then you are OK. If not, you have an out.
3. Make your offers qualified offers. That is, "We could quote if..." This gives you much more freedom and flexibility.

Today almost everyone uses e-mail on a regular basis. I have a six-year-old grandson who is very good on the computer. We are all very comfortable with it. For some young people, this is all they know. It is very easy to negotiate using e-mail, if the other side suggests it. Please be very careful. It is my opinion that it is best not to negotiate using only e-mail.

Face-to-face is the very best way to negotiate. Second best is on the telephone, with a written follow-up. The last best is using e-mails or other forms of written communications.

Conclusion

The purpose of this final chapter is twofold: first, to take a long summary look at the negotiation process, and second, to review a few positive behaviors of savvy negotiators.

THE NEGOTIATION PROCESS

The negotiation process provides people with a process that will resolve differences between people without fighting. It provides an opportunity to improve their lives and their organization's success. It is a process that each person must become better at, because we negotiate every day at work, in our communities, and in our homes.

At a very basic level, negotiation is the opposite of fighting or using force to obtain your objectives. The negotiation process allows two (or more) sides to come together in an agreement for a future relationship based on consent, not fear. Too often people (especially the media) with little knowledge of the process use words that make us think of war such as "fighting it out," "winning key concessions," "giving away important issues," and "losing the negotiation."

In my classes, I ask the students (working in groups) to list all the ways to resolve conflict. Each group develops a list of twenty to thirty options such as these:

1. Walk away
2. Toss a coin
3. Give in

4. Go to court
5. Take to a higher level

They also list extreme options such as these:

6. Intimidate
7. Punish
8. Hurt
9. Kill

In fact, all are options that will resolve conflict, even ones we may not chose to take. (Note: killing the other person will in fact resolve the conflict between two people. It just develops another area of conflict.) Then we have a long class discussion that determines that almost every option for resolving conflict is a win-lose option except negotiation, which is the best way to resolve conflict and have a win-win agreement.

Also, in my classes I review the differences between sports and negotiations so that my students obtain a better understanding of the negotiation process. There are nine differences:

1. Games have time limits; negotiations do not have time limits.
2. Games have rules; negotiations do not have rules.
3. Games do not address needs; negotiations always address needs.
4. In games we react; in negotiations we proact (that is, make offers).
5. In games there are fixed values (touchdown, six points); each issue has many values during the negotiation.
6. In games you know the amount of risk versus reward; in negotiations you don't.
7. Games have scoreboards; no scoreboards for negotiation.
8. When the game is over, the score can't be changed; negotiators can get even after a negotiation.
9. Games have one winner; negotiations must have two winners.

The negotiation process allows people that are weaker than their opponents to be able to settle differences and obtain their needs or wants. This is a major advantage we have as people. In the animal world, the rule is survival of the fittest. The weak animals are the ones that predators attack and kill. Again, since negotiation is aimed at satisfying needs, the stronger person has a strong interest in negotiating a deal with the weaker person.

Before a negotiation starts, several conditions must exist:

1. There must be a desire on each side to negotiate.
2. The items being negotiated must be in shortsupply. That is, the items can't be easily obtained without the negotiation. This relates to all items, both tangible (cars, houses, money, etc.) and intangible (services, time, advice, etc.).
3. The items must really be negotiable.
4. The needs or wants must overlap so that there is an area in which to negotiate.
5. The needs or wants must be different. That is, if both sides have all the same needs, there is no area in which to negotiate.
6. Both sides have an objective of reaching an acceptable agreement.

Everyone negotiates! As soon as babies can communicate, they start using the negotiation process. Most of the time this is before they can walk or talk. A baby can cry! Unless there is a medical problem, crying becomes a negotiation tactic for babies. They try to get their way by negotiating and bargaining with their parents and other family members. For example, a child may say, "Can I stay up an extra half an hour tonight if I'm good?" The child is offering value (being good) if the parent offers value (staying up an extra half hour). This is a classic negotiation situation. The parents may accept or they may make the stakes higher by saying, "Yes, if you also eat all your dinner." When the child says yes, the negotiation has been finished with a win-win outcome. Both sides have given and received value.

I've found that children are very good negotiators. Why? Because they do not have the financial resources, the physical resources, nor the educational resources to live on their own. The child needs the parent to provide many resources (food, shelter, clothes, etc.), so the child must learn to negotiate to satisfy his or her needs. For example, picture your local grocery store. A twenty-seven-year-old human being is pushing a grocery cart. In the cart is a three-year-old human being. Which human being has more physical power? The twenty-seven-year-old. Which human being has more education? The twenty-seven-year-old. Which human being has more financial power? The twenty-seven-year-old. Which human being wins the negotiation concerning the candy bar in the rack at the checkout station? The three-year-old!

Two short examples from the newspapers provide insight into our motivation to negotiate. A *Family Circus* cartoon featured the older brother saying to the younger one, "Ask Mommy for ten cookies, but then tell her you'll settle for two." The May 23, 2004, *San Jose Mercury News* included a quote from pitcher Miguel Batista on learning a new language in the minor leagues: "When you tell a guy you have to go take an English class to learn how to say this, how to say that it's difficult. When you tell a guy, go ahead because she's going to teach you how to talk to a girl, everybody wants to go."

From an early age until death, people negotiate their way through life. They negotiate with their parents, their family, their friends, their peers, their bosses, their subordinates, their counterparts in business (buyer or seller, management or union, etc.), for their personal purchases, and so on.

POSITIVE NEGOTIATION BEHAVORS

Several studies of the behaviors of successful negotiators list many common behaviors. They are listed here for the reader's review and personal development. Successful, savvy negotiators:

1. Are confident people who concentrate on the issues and do not attack their opponents.
2. Do not get into the very destructive circle of attacking the other side when they are attacked. Poor negotiators fall into the trap of defending themselves by attacking their opponent. As the attacks continue, they become increasingly malicious. Instead of discussing issues, the negotiation becomes a contest to see who can hurt the other person the most.
3. Do not use dirty tricks and see the use of these trick as a sign of weakness.
4. Have the skills to overcome opponents who do use dirty tricks.
5. Use questions for many purposes (see chapter 3). Research has shown that successful negotiators ask twice as many questions as poor negotiators do.
6. Use objective words, not subjective words. In my classes I use this example: "What is a fair price?" There is a long discussion that becomes heated at times because everyone has their own opinion of a fair price. Then I teach that successful, savvy negotiators use objective words such as an *acceptable price*.

7. Are able to test their assumptions during the negotiation process. During the planning of a negotiation, we must make assumptions about the other side. For example, if a buyer is planning to ask the seller to stock material for the buyer, the buyer has to make an assumption about the cost of money for the seller. During the negotiation, the buyer must probe to determine the actual cost of money.

8. Are able to test for understanding and agreement. The successful person asks questions to ensure that the opponent understands what is being agreed to, before they shake hands. If one side doesn't understand what they really are committed to do, the deal will fall apart. The successful person always remembers that we negotiate to set the ground rules for a future relationship.

9. Generally delay areas of disagreement until later in the negotiation. They look for areas of agreement to build on. They hope to be able to say, "Look, we have agreed on all these points; we should be able to reach a compromise on these last few points.

TWO IMPORTANT BEHAVIORS FOR SUCESSFUL NEGOTIATORS

There are two final learning objectives for this book. The first is that the savvy negotiator must operate on two different levels at the same time. First, the negotiator must be able to be "above" the negotiation looking "down" at the negotiating table, objectively watching what is going on. The negotiator must analyze the situation in great depth to see how a win-win outcome can be achieved. Detachment allows the savvy negotiator to understand the other side and their needs. The perfect way to achieve detachment is to imagine that you are an independent third party who has no stake in the outcome of the negotiation. When you can do this, you will have a tremendous advantage over your opponent. You will be able to control the negotiation and you will be able to satisfy your needs.

At the same time, of course, you must be on one side of the table, negotiating with your opponent to achieve your and your principal's needs.

The successful negotiator understands that there are really three positions at every negotiation table. There is position A (your side of the table), position B (your opponent's side of the table), and position C (above the table objectively watching and evaluating). The side that occupies position C is the side that will win almost all of their negotiations. This is very hard to do, as most people get so involved in the negotiation that they forget everything else. The savvy negotiator will work very hard at developing this skill.

> **Key to Success:** Always Work on Two Levels during Every Negotiation

The final learning objective is this: the savvy negotiator never lets the negotiation become a zero-sum negotiation.

> **Key to Success:** Never Let the Negotiation Become a Zero-Sum Negotiation

Appendix: Keys to Success

Listed below are the keys to success included in this book. These seventy-one keys are listed in the same order as they were discussed in the text. There is no priority, because each one is very important for success.

THE FOUR TRUTHS OF TWENTY-FIRST-CENTURY NEGOTIATIONS

1. The purpose of negotiations is to set the ground rules for a future relationship.
2. The objective of negotiations is to find a win-win outcome.
3. The reason for negotiations is to satisfy needs on both sides of the negotiation table.
4. Negotiators must be evaluated by the results of the relationships formed by the negotiation, not just the negotiation itself.

KEYS TO SUCCESS

Chapter 2

Win relationships, not negotiations.
Professional behavior gets positive results.
Remember, you negotiate to satisfy your needs.
Satisfy your opponent's needs first.
Buy when you do not have to buy.
Start with low offers.

You lose nothing by asking.
You never get more than you ask for.
Do not take rejection as a personal rejection.
Do not make a rejection feel like a personal rejection.
Let the other side make the first proposal.

Chapter 3

Don't answer your own questions.
Don't ask yes-or-no questions.
The side that asks the most questions does best.
The side that answers the most questions does worst.
You must get information and commitment to be successful.
The side that talks the least usually does the best.
Remember that we have two ears and one mouth.
You have a lot of power when you answer a question.
Before you answer a hard question, determine whether you want a conflict or a
    compromise.
Very bad questions can be answered yes or no.
Be patient when asking questions.
Understand slow human responses.
Know when to stop asking questions.
Help the other person when you give your answer.
Be the last seller to negotiate with the buyer.
Sell product differentiation whenever possible.
Sit at the head of the negotiation table.
If not at the head, sit at the foot of the table.
First control the situation, then go for the win-win.
Put time limits on the other side.
Use if-questions to get firm commitments from others.
Never give a firm commitment to an if-question.
Negotiate at your opponent's need level.
Separate needs from wants.
Questions are a good way to test asumptions.
Questions can help to avoid conflict.
Use "I don't understand" to get more information.
Hear what is not said.
Write out questions before negotiating.
Always avoid a quick response.

Chapter 4

Always read the eyes of your opponent.
Be aware of the quick close.
There is no free lunch.
If it seems too good to be true, it is.
Be aware of the loss leader.
Be aware of bait-and-switch tactics.
Take the Morrison Mirror Test when you retire.
Pass the Morrison Mirror Quiz each week.
Ethical behavior is a must in all negotiations.

Chapter 5

Focus on real, provable accomplishments.
Keep a detailed brag file for raise and promotion negotiations.
Keep emotions out of home purchase negotiations.
Location and market timing are critical to the final price.
Understand the agent's true objectives.
Negotiate all issues when buying or selling a home.
To save money, beware of car sellers' negotiation tactics.
Many hotel discounts are available—just ask.
At hotels, ask for rates and availability.
Call direct to the hotel, not a national 800 number.
There are many ways to save money at a hotel, so ask.
There are many items to be negotiated with airlines.
There is no "I" in a family "team."
Consider all options before making a decision.
Keep emotions out of negotiations.
The most important point to remember in all family and friend negotiations
    is to look for a win-win outcome.
Never make the most important person in your life be a loser.
Never make the other important people in your life be losers.
Almost every life situation is a negotiation situation.
Never sell yourself short.
Future business is an important leverage point.

Chapter 6

Always confirm phone negotiations in writing.
Always know who you are negotiating with.

Ask opponents to restate their statements, not repeat.
"Hmmm" is not acceptance.
Never negotiate while driving.

Conclusion

Always work on two levels during every negotiation.
Never let the negotiation become a zero-sum negotiation.

The final key to success is to remember that in almost every case, we are negotiating with a person or company with whom we will have an ongoing relationship. We must always focus on the relationship, not just the negotiation.

We Negotiate to Set the Ground Rules for a Future Relationship

We Must Win Relationships, Not Just Negotiations

The purpose of this book will be realized when you remember these final two keys to success and use the other keys during all your negotiations—both business and personal.

Notes

CHAPTER 1

1. W. Morrison, *Negotiation in the Twenty-first Century*, paper presented at the fourteenth annual CSU-POM conference, San Jose State University, February 22–23, 2002.

2. Ricky W. Griffin and Ronald J. Ebert, *Business*, 5th ed. (Upper Saddle River, NJ: Prentice Hall, 1999), 247.

3. Michiel R. Leenders and Harold E. Fearon, *Purchasing and Supply Management*, 11th ed. (Chicago: Irwin, 1997), 325, 326, 351.

CHAPTER 6

1. Chester Karrass, *Traffic Management* (1995, November): 34.

2. Max H. Bazerman, *Annual Review of Psychology* (2000).

Index

About the Author

WILLIAM F. MORRISON is a lecturer in the Department of Organization and Management in the College of Business, San Jose State University, where he teaches courses in negotiation, management, and operations. He has also taught at Golden Gate University, the University of California-Berkeley, and Menlo College. The author of two books on negotiation—*The Prenegotiation Planning Book* and *The Human Side of Negotiations*—he served in management positions at Westinghouse for 37 years and currently conducts negotiation and management training programs for corporations and industry groups.